PENGUIN BOOKS

RUN OR DIE

RUN
KILIAN JORNET
OR DIE

TRANSLATED FROM CATALAN
BY PETER BUSH

PENGUIN BOOKS

PENGUIN BOOKS

Published by the Penguin Group
Penguin Books Ltd, 80 Strand, London WC2R 0RL, England
Penguin Group (USA) Inc., 375 Hudson Street, New York, New York 10014, USA
Penguin Group (Canada), 90 Eglinton Avenue East, Suite 700, Toronto, Ontario, Canada M4P 2Y3
(a division of Pearson Penguin Canada Inc.)
Penguin Ireland, 25 St Stephen's Green, Dublin 2, Ireland (a division of Penguin Books Ltd)
Penguin Group (Australia), 707 Collins Street, Melbourne, Victoria 3008, Australia
(a division of Pearson Australia Group Pty Ltd)
Penguin Books India Pvt Ltd, 11 Community Centre, Panchsheel Park, New Delhi – 110 017, India
Penguin Group (NZ), 67 Apollo Drive, Rosedale, Auckland 0632, New Zealand
(a division of Pearson New Zealand Ltd)
Penguin Books (South Africa) (Pty) Ltd, Block D, Rosebank Office Park,
181 Jan Smuts Avenue, Parktown North, Gauteng 2193, South Africa

Penguin Books Ltd, Registered Offices: 80 Strand, London WC2R 0RL, England

www.penguin.com

First published as *Córrer o Morir* in Spain by Ara Llibres SCCL 2011
This translation first published in the USA by VeloPress 2013
Published in Penguin Books 2014
001

ISBN: 978–0–241–00485–2

www.greenpenguin.co.uk

To Núria, for showing me the way
and lighting it when it gets dark

CONTENTS

The Skyrunner's Manifesto   viii

1 | What Do You Want to Be When You Grow Up?   1

2 | Adrenaline Comes with a Number   19

3 | It's Not Only About Competing   41

4 | The Windy City   65

5 | Lakes, Rivers, and Rain   99

6 | A Victory for the Senses   119

7 | Running a Long Way to Find Yourself   131

8 | We Celebrate a Peak When We're Back Down   151

9 | What I Think About When I Think About Running   171

Acknowledgments   181

Credits   182

THE SKYRUNNER'S MANIFESTO

Kiss or kill. Besa o mata. *Kiss glory or die in the attempt. Losing is death; winning is life. The fight is what decides the victory, the winner. How often have rage and pain made you cry? How often has exhaustion made you lose your memory, voice, common sense? And how often in this state have you exclaimed, with a broad smile on your face, "The final stage! Two more hours! Go, onward and upward! That pain only exists inside your head. Control it, destroy it, eliminate it, and keep on. Make your rivals suffer. Kill them." I am selfish, right? Sport is selfish, because you must be selfish to know how to fight on while you suffer, to love solitude and hell. Stopping, coughing, feeling cold, not feeling your legs, feeling sick, vomiting, getting headaches, cuts, bleeding . . . can you think of anything better?*

The secret isn't in your legs, but in your strength of mind. You need to go for a run when it is raining, windy, and snowing, when lightning sets trees on fire as you pass them, when snowflakes or hailstones strike your legs and body in the storm and make you weep, and in order to keep running, you have to wipe away the tears to see the stones, walls, or sky. The strength of mind to say no to hours of partying, to good grades, to a pretty girl, to the bedsheets against your face. To put your soul into it, going out into the rain until your legs bleed from the cuts when you slip on the mud and fall to the ground, and then get back on your feet and continue uphill until your legs cry out, "Enough!" and leave you marooned in a storm on the remotest peaks, until you die.

Leggings soaked by snow, driven on by the wind that sticks to your face and freezes your sweat. Feeling the pressure from your legs, the weight of your body bearing down on the metatarsals in your toes, pressure that can shatter rocks, destroy planets, and move continents. Legs suspended in the air, gliding like an eagle, or running faster than a cheetah. Running downhill, slipping on the snow and mud before driving yourself on anew, and suddenly you are free to fly, to shout out in the heart of the mountain, with only the most intrepid rodents and birds hidden in their nests beneath the rocks as your confessors. Only they know your secrets, your fears. Because losing is death. And you should not die before you have given your all, have wept from the pain and the wounds. And you cannot surrender. You must fight on to the death. Because glory is the greatest, and you can either aspire to glory or fall by the wayside. You cannot simply not fight, not suffer, not die. . . . Now is the time to suffer, the time to fight, the time to win. Kiss or kill.

Pinned on the door of an old flat, these were the words I read every morning before I went out training.

what do you want to be when you grow up?

1

want to count lakes when I grow up. I want to be a counter of lakes!"

The teacher turned around from the blackboard, where she was chalking up a list of the professions we wanted to enter when we grew up, and stared at me.

"That's right, a counter of lakes. But I don't just want to count how many there are. I want to walk in the mountains, and when I find a lake, I will find out how deep it is by throwing in a stone attached to a piece of rope. I want to find out how long and wide it is. I want to find out if it has fish, frogs, or tadpoles. And if the water is clean or not."

The teacher looked even more taken aback, since that isn't the job most 5-year-olds want, but I was really very determined. It was to be my destiny.

Add to that the fact that I always, as long as I can remember, came back from every climb and hike with, at the very least, a stone from the peak or the highest point we reached—a custom I still keep. I collect all types and colors of stone: volcanic rock from Mount Kilimanjaro and the Garrotxa, granite from the Alps and the Pyrenees, ocher from Morocco and Cappadocia, blue stone from Erciyes, slate from Cerro Plata. . . . I think I must have been predestined to be a geologist or a geographer. Predestined to discover the secrets of the earth by searching for stones on every peak and in every cave, to explore its landscapes and reveal how the earth had been able to raise constructions as complex as sierras, with their mountains, valleys, and lakes, all of it working together perfectly, like a Swiss watch, and nothing or no one, not even the most powerful of men, able to stifle their rhythm and power.

I think that occasion was one of the few when I have said, "I want to be." I've always been the kind of person who prefers to say, "I'll try." I have always been shy and have always thought it best to let time go by, that in the end things will find their rightful place. And in the end, they have.

I enjoyed a normal childhood. I spent my time out of school playing near my parents' house by myself or with my sister or school friends. We played tag and hide-and-seek, built huts and fortresses, and transformed our space into imaginary scenes from films or comics. I have never been one to like being shut inside and was lucky that my parents lived in a mountain refuge, which my father managed, 6,500 feet above sea level, on the northern slopes of Cerdanya, between the mountain frontiers with France and Andorra. My playground was never a street or a backyard; it was the woods on Cap del Rec, the cross-country ski runs and peaks of Tossa Plana, the river Muga, and Port de Perafita pass. That was where I began to discover the fascinating world of nature.

When we got home from school, we didn't even take time to drop off our backpacks in the dining room because we immediately started climbing rocks or hanging off the branches of a tree in summer or leaping over snow-covered fields on cross-country skis in winter.

Every evening before going to sleep, my sister, mother, and I would go out in our pajamas for a walk in the woods in the dark, without headlamps. We deliberately kept off paths, and thus when our eyes adapted to the dark and our ears to the silence, we were gradually able to hear how the woods breathed and to "see" the ground through our feet. We overrate our sense of sight, and when we lose it, we feel unprotected and exposed to the dangers in the world outside. But what danger can you encounter in the woods in the Pyrenees at night? The only natural predators—wolves and bears—have been few and far between for years. As for other animals, what danger is there if you walk by a fox or a hare, given that you are an animal 10 or 15 times its size? And what about the trees? Your ears learn to hear the wind rustling their leaves, and that is how you are able to see them. And the ground? Your feet tell you if there are branches, grass, mud, or water, if it goes up or down, or if there's a sudden rush of water.

And that's how our time flew by, between games played near the refuge and weekend and holiday excursions. Whenever we had two or three free days, we made the most of them to explore a new mountain. When we were starting to walk, we climbed the peaks closest to home and then gradually sought out new, more distant adventures. By the age of 3 I had already climbed Tossa Plana, Perafita, and La Muga. By age 6 I had completed four Aneto summits, and at age 10 I crossed the Pyrenees in 42 days. However, on these excursions we never simply followed the footsteps of our parents. They took us to the top and were our guides, but we had to find the path, look for the signs, and understand why a path went this way and not that. We weren't passive observers of what was happening around us. The mountain took on a broader meaning than the space where we usually played. It was terrain with a life of its own, and we had to get to know it so that we could explore it safely and anticipate the dangers. We had to adapt to the terrain where we were born. This was how our parents taught us to love the mountains: They made us feel like part of them. Because, in essence, mountains are like people: To love them, you must first get to know them, and when you do, you can tell when they are angry and when they are happy, how you should handle them, play with them, care for them when people hurt them, when it is better not to annoy them. But unlike any person, the mountains, nature, and the earth are much, much bigger than you are. You must never forget that you are a speck, a speck in space, within the infinite, and they can decide at any moment whether they want to erase that speck or not.

When I was 8, I went on a trip that became etched in my memory, and one that I often remember when I am running.

We took the train to A Coruña. The weather was cool, and although it wasn't raining, it seemed likely that the first drops would fall at any moment. We took our bicycles off the train and started to pedal. I rode my mother's mountain bike. It was very new, and although my feet barely reached the pedals, the brightly colored decorations on the spokes of both wheels meant that we were inseparable. My sister, Naila, was 7, and she had had her own bike for three years. Although the bike was still in perfect condition, Naila had grown over those years and now had to pedal very quickly to keep up speed. My mother rode an old Peugeot road bike with the gear change on the handlebars and carried a large backpack over the back wheel with everything the three of us might need on a week spent sleeping and pedaling in Galicia.

We rode out to the south and made good progress with few problems and at a decent enough speed. I rode in front on that huge bike, Naila rode behind me pedaling frantically, and my mother drifted between us, making sure we were each okay.

We rode to Santiago de Compostela in a drizzly mist that left us soaked for the whole day. On one of our stops, when she was looking at an ancient Michelin road map, my mother pointed to the white line along the side of the road and said, "Kilian, you must follow this line, and don't leave it at any crossroads, since there will be a road that continues to the right. Okay?"

I understood her perfectly and started pedaling, focusing on that white line on a bendy stretch of road, while my mother followed a long way behind with Naila. The crossroads started to come, cars overtook me on my right and left, and buses and trucks honked and roared at me. But I faithfully followed the signs and made sure I kept to the white line. All of a sudden I saw my mother running with her bicycle on the side of the road. She was shouting at me to get away from the middle of the road.

"Kilian, what on earth do you think you're doing? Get out of the middle of the road!"

As a result of how the roads were painted, the line I was following led straight into the second lane of traffic on the main road going into Santiago. And I had clung to my mother's words and hadn't left it for an inch. I rode over to where my mother was standing, sweating from the effort she'd expended. She hugged me, then got started repairing the wheel that had been punctured when she was chasing after me.

The next three days were a hard struggle against a fierce north wind. We followed the ups and downs of the coastal roads, with the wind constantly driving us back. Naila strained to ride uphill on her small bike as I galloped ahead at top speed, and my mother did her best to keep an eye on both of us. Nevertheless, we reached Cape Finisterre on an evening with light clouds and a cool breeze in time to see a beautiful sunset over the sea on the horizon.

We had forgotten to take into account that the light would disappear quickly when the sun went down. As usual, we rode off as fast as we could, and all I had buzzing in my head was something my mother had said: "Stop at the campsite with green doors and two flags flying. Naila and I will catch up with you."

I started to pedal as quickly as my legs would allow and began to eat up the miles. On my right, the beaches started to disappear and were replaced by mountains. *How strange. I thought the site was much nearer*, I kept thinking as night fell and the road climbed higher and higher. I reached the mountain pass and began to ride down the other side. There were no lights in front or to my right and no sign pointing to a campsite farther on. I accelerated to get there faster. It started to get cold, and I felt sleepy. All of a sudden as I rounded a bend, a small red car overtook me and came to a halt. A small, tubby man got out of the driver's door, shaking with laughter. My mother got out of the other door, still wearing her cycling shoes.

"Didn't you see the campsite?" she scolded me.

"Hmm . . . no, I didn't see any sign of it. I've seen only beaches and then mountains," I said, thinking back to everything I'd seen since I'd started pedaling.

"And on your left?" she asked, looking at me incredulously.

I felt so stupid. There'd been a 50 percent chance that the campsite would be on the left of the road, but that had never struck me. I smiled, laughing at myself, and climbed into the car belonging to the owner of the campsite, who drove us to the tent where Naila was cooking dinner.

In the morning we got up early in order to reach A Coruña in the afternoon. This time we set off together to avoid more mishaps, but on the last climb before we reached the city, my mother's bike decided that it had had enough, that it had fought too many battles, and its chain and gears jammed. As we hadn't included any tools for bike repair in our backpack, we had to go to a small village shop to buy oil.

After several attempts, moving everything we could with our hands, we managed to sort the chain out, but the bike was left with a fixed wheel. Unless she wanted her legs to look like they were powering a dryer on express cycle, she had to put them on her handlebars when we went downhill. Naila and I rode behind her to ensure there was no accident.

We stayed overnight in a small hotel in the city center and the following morning got up early to catch the train. At the start of our journey we had had problems transporting our bikes, so this time we wrapped them up at the hotel. We didn't have any large bags or cardboard boxes, so we had to put them in our sleeping bags. The only snag with this well-rehearsed solution was the question of how were we going to transport them to the station, since my sister and I were unable to carry parcels that were bigger than we were. We decided on the following method: I accompanied my mother halfway with one bike. She went back for the other bike and in two trips got the bike and Naila. We then repeated the process from the city center to the train station.

Our honesty prevented my sister and me from earning our first wage that day. When people walked past us and saw a boy or girl alone, face exhausted after so many days of hard toil, clothes dirty with oil from bike chains, sitting next to a large sleeping bag, they felt sorry and offered us money so that we could buy food. We stared at them in amazement, not understanding what made them think we were hungry, as we had eaten breakfast only a few hours before. Naturally, we refused their money.

We finally reached the train station, where, on the inspector's orders, we had to remove the bikes from our sleeping bags and stay by the door area and move them from right to left so that people could get in and out at each station. After a few hours a female conductor took pity on us and let us put our bikes in the room where they stored train equipment, and then we managed to sleep until we arrived home.

Our excursions went from games to activities and then to sport. Competition came onto the scene when I started high school and enrolled at the Center for Mountain Skiing Skills to use up some of my excess energy. Training began, with races here, there, and everywhere—first across the Pyrenees and later on throughout Europe. My first race results brought with them the desire to do better. Helped by Maite Hernández, Jordi Canals, and the whole team at the center, as well as by my mother, who drove me everywhere to train in the early morning before going to school, it seemed that I had started on my career and that my most important successes must still lie ahead, even though I had won everything at the junior level.

But life always places obstacles in our way. December 22, 2006, was the morning after winning what was at that time my goal in life, the Agustí Roca, for the first time. As I was going home from school, I jumped from one road to another as I had done so often before, but this time my feet didn't coordinate and I crashed to the ground. I felt a searing pain in my left knee and right hand.

I limped home as best I could and sat on the sofa, waiting for the inflammation to go away and for the pain to lessen. Quite the reverse happened: By the time it was dark, my knee was so swollen that my parents took me to the hospital, albeit reluctantly.

"You've broken your kneecap and the metacarpals of your right hand," said the doctor. As she uttered these words, my world started to collapse around me. "It would be best, ideally as soon as possible, to operate and insert a metal plate. Hopefully, it will make you as good as new."

It was a difficult decision, and at that moment I was unable to think very clearly. I was at a high point in my short sporting career, and as a mere 18-year-old, I couldn't see any way forward. Was my career at an end? Would I recover from this injury? I could no doubt take up sport again, but would I return to the level I had fought so hard to reach? I wanted answers, and answers now. I couldn't imagine spending a year not competing and not training. What should I do? These unanswered questions continued to trouble me even as I went into the operating room so that they could put a metal plate around my kneecap.

I decided I would have to look for other solutions. If I couldn't compete at the same high level, I would have to find other goals and motivations to fight for. Consequently, in the three months I was in bed in a cast, I tried to find out all I could about mountain skiing. I looked at studies and experiments in technique carried out in the area of cross-country skiing in order to apply them to my sport. I read books on sporting psychology for ways to improve my tactics. I spent nights in front of a computer surfing pages on physiology and sport strategies in order to extend my understanding of my body and avoid sleepless nights with too many unanswered questions.

I went to the hospital in March to have the cast removed. I was very disappointed when I saw my leg for the first time after so long. No, that wasn't my leg! It couldn't be! Mine was muscular and strong. That scrap of hairy flesh couldn't be mine! Good heavens! Then I got very gloomy. By way of consolation, I reminded myself that at least with the knowledge I'd acquired over the last three months of intensive research, I could continue with some kind of link to the world of sport.

The first sessions with the physiotherapist were horrible. I was unable to move my leg without electrostimulation; I was unable to stand up straight without the help of a cane. How would I ever run again if I couldn't stand up straight? However, I gradually improved and my leg began to get stronger. Within a week I could stand up without the cane, and if I could stand up, I could stand up on skis, right? I tried to. I went to the ski slopes and put boots on for the first time in four months. I knew that my doctors wouldn't be pleased to know I was skiing, but in the end I was simply standing up, with the boots supporting my feet. It was like being at home and doing physical exercise.

I started to go up slopes, and though I was in terrible shape, I realized that I could do it, that I could do what I used to do, and I felt the adrenaline spreading through my veins. I reached the top of the slopes as excited as someone who had just won a medal in the Olympics. I started to sing, dance, and shout as if I were alone in the world. The skiers around me stared at me as if I had gone crazy. In fact, after so many months of making no effort at all, I really must have suffered a wholesale destruction of my neurons. After that first rush of adrenaline, I calmed down and asked myself a basic question: *How the hell am I going to get down?* I was so excited to discover that I could ski again that I hadn't thought about how I would get down after I'd climbed the slope. I started my descent on the shoulders of a friend who volunteered his back to support my weight. Halfway down we realized that wasn't the best solution, so I continued my descent using only one leg—my good one, of course—with the frail one doubled under me so that it didn't touch the ground.

From then on I had only one aim in mind: to persuade my doctors and physiotherapists that I could start training. It was difficult initially. When I smiled broadly and told the doctor I had been skiing and that it had turned out very well, her reply was clear and no-nonsense:

"I'll put you back in a cast!"

"No, no, please, I'll be a good boy. I'll do whatever I have to. Gym, swimming pool, physio . . . but no more casts, please!"

When I saw that the medical route was completely blocked, I focused instead on my physiotherapist. He told me that when I could bend my leg 90 degrees, I could start on a stationary bike, and that in the meantime I should go to the swimming pool and walk underwater. From then on I did all I could to bend my leg. I sat on it to put pressure on it, used weights to make the joint more flexible, and made a few degrees of progress. I went once to the swimming pool, but walking around in a pool full of senior citizens wasn't the most entertaining activity in the world.

I concluded that I could reinterpret the physiotherapist's words. He had suggested walking in water. A swimming pool is water, and water and snow are more or less the same thing, if only in a different state, right? Was I to blame if physics played these tricks? So I walked in snow, with skis on my feet, for three weeks until I reached the longed-for 90 degrees and could mount a stationary bike. The first session went very well, and the physiotherapist said I could go to the gym in Puigcerdà for sessions on a stationary bike.

I went to the gym, got on the bike, and stuck at it for 15 minutes while watching video clips on the TV screen in front of the bike, and came to the conclusion that 90 degrees are 90 degrees whether on a stationary bike or on a road bike. I looked outside; it was sunny and warm. I went home, grabbed my bike, and went for a real ride, one mountain pass after another. That is how I started to alternate trips out on my skis and on my bike. So, in essence, I did everything I was told to do: walk in water and ride a bike. It was simply better not to mention the context if I was ever asked. I had my first problem when the doctor saw the results table from the Catalan Cross-Country Skiing Championship.

"It just happened to be near our house," I replied, head bowed but unable to repress a smile. "I went over to check out the atmosphere, and as I'd done well the previous year, it turned out they had a number for me, and I can never say no and accepted. I started at a steady pace, not intending to finish the race, but it was easier to finish than to get to the top by car, because the roads are in such bad shape. However, I came down using only one leg. . . ."

"Well, as there's nothing I can do to stop you," she said, "at least make sure you don't fall until we remove the metal plate from your knee."

And with that carte blanche I began to train like a trouper and gradually not only got back to the level I had enjoyed before that wretched fall, but even improved on it.

A day comes in life when you have to decide which train to take, and once you are aboard, there is no point in thinking what might have happened if you had caught a different one. You have to make the most of what you find on your route. We can never know what the other trains have to offer, even though we lie awake many a night dreaming that they are better. In truth, perfection only exists within us, in what we think is perfect. Each track leads us to a different place, but it is *our* choices that lead us to find moments of happiness on any particular track.

At age 18 we all reach a decision point: You must choose a career, a car, an apartment to live in, a bank account; whether you want to have a family, pets, kitchen furniture, cutlery, and napkins; must decide on a television channel you want to watch, a contract for a cell phone, what to eat for lunch, how to kill time on a Sunday afternoon. Choose your future; choose a life. However, I decided to choose none of that. I chose a different kind of life.

I lived in a 194-square-foot studio in the Grand Hotel in Font-Romeu. I lived with a friend, although there were usually five or six people sleeping on our floor. It was on the ground floor of a huge building that dated from the beginning of the last century and that looked down on the back of Font-Romeu. The room was on the right of a large hall with winding stairs and marble banisters that showed they had once belonged to the glories of the French bourgeoisie, although it was now dark, uninhabited, and more like an imitation of the hotel in *The Shining*. The door was made from sturdy wood and was painted a nondescript color, paint that was beginning to flake. The small gilt plate on the door, inscribed with the number 18 and redone with a marker, was the only feature to distinguish my room from the more than 50 doors on that wing of the building.

Once inside, on the left was a toilet separated off by a sliding door and on the right a bathroom with a sink, mirror, and small bath in which there was only enough space to stand up. The room was square, with a single window that made up the whole northern side and that was often left ajar in anticipation of days when we returned home and the doors were locked and we'd mislaid our keys—something that happened often. A thick blue carpet covered the floor, and the only piece of furniture was a bunk bed fixed to the left wall. On the right were a small freezer (rarely full) and the stove, with three burners and an oven in which we kept two saucepans, a frying pan, and an iron. Next to the burners you could usually find a box of chocolate cereal, packages of cookies, some boxes of spaghetti and macaroni, a salt cellar, a pot of oregano, a bottle of olive oil, two jars of tomato paste, and a packet of grated cheese. These were the ingredients that made up our diet. In fact, what we usually cooked was a saucepan of pasta with tomato sauce that we reheated whenever we got back from training and felt our strength was fading. It was vital to consume as many calories as possible in order to keep running as long as possible.

Facing the bunk beds, on a chair, was a small television set that always carried the same DVD, *The Technique of Champions*, featuring footage and technical sequences of the greatest ski mountaineers of the moment. Before we went out to train, a video session motivated us to give 200 percent and try to imitate the turns of Stéphane Brosse or the audacious skiing of Guido Giacomelli.

Our clothes were piled on the floor, lined up in two rows. At the back, pants, T-shirts, and sweaters for normal wear, and in front our training gear, skiing overalls, thermal shirts, pants, leggings, gloves, caps. Next to our clothes were our tool kit, the iron, wax for the skis, scissors, cutters, bits from all kinds of televisions, and cord and string, with which we built and destroyed, made and unmade all the equipment we had. The rest of the room was taken up by what we called "our first girlfriends": bikes, trainers, boots, and skis that received preferential treatment in the studio apartment. We hung a poster of the 20th edition of Pierre Menta on the wall, a mountain skiing race for teams of two that lasts for four days and is known as the Tour de France of mountain skiing, the race won by the greatest mountain skiers in the world, the race you had to compete in at least once in your life, the race we dreamed about day after day as we trained, slept, and ate. We hung the Skyrunner's Manifesto on the back of the front door, a declaration that gave us the strength to keep going as long as we could in adverse weather conditions.

That is how, between those four walls, joined by our deep desire to destroy our bodies through hours and hours of training, Fuenri's Factory was born. A group of friends with just two ideas in their heads: miles and yet more miles. Nothing else mattered. Where or how you slept, what you ate or, if necessary, did not eat. What mattered was to train and compete to the maximum.

I remember leaving home on my bike with my skis tied to my backpack and riding 37 miles to reach the snow, skiing until it was dark, and then returning home at night, my headlamp frozen. I remember setting up a tent in the car park in Astun the night before the Spanish championships and waking up to 5°F and not being able to take down the tent because it was frozen to the ground. I remember lots of Saturday nights sleeping in the car or with my boots in a sleeping bag in order to compete on Sunday.

Our whole lives revolved around competition. We slept and ate enough to be able to train, and we trained to the maximum to be able to compete and try to get the best results possible. All our income, which came from study grants and race prizes, went toward paying the rent and buying the best gear—gear that we then took apart in our workshop to make it as light as possible, with the obvious consequences. We kept changing shops to buy our boots, since we were embarrassed to go into the same shop for the fourth week in a row to buy yet another pair of boots.

The climax came one Wednesday in March. We had no electricity in the studio, since we had decided it was more important to have a good pair of carbonite ski poles than electricity. Álvaro, my roommate and racing partner, and I were sitting on the floor with the rent for the month scattered over the carpet, wondering if it was more important to give the rent to Madame Levy, our landlady, or to leave that afternoon for Arêches Beaufort, the center of the world as far as we were concerned, and where the Pierre Menta was to start the following morning.

Obviously, we both knew what we would decide, and so within minutes we were loading our bags and skis into our white Peugeot Partner. We picked up my sister, Naila, and my best girlfriend, Mireia, and set out on the highway until we reached Arêches seven hours later. That was when the real odyssey started: convincing the organization to let us take part. Registering for the race was highly competitive, and even though we wanted to race in the junior category, places were restricted and had been filled some time ago. However, we didn't give up hope, and after spending hours going to and fro and talking to all the organizers, we finally got a number. Our number to take part in the Pierre Menta! Our dream began there. We slept in the girls' room, since we'd spent our rent money on registering and couldn't allow ourselves to spend more money on a hotel. The race was wonderful: an incredible atmosphere, good vibes, a victory on Sunday and a second-place finish in the general race for youngsters, and, above all, the adrenaline of waking up in the morning knowing that only one thing mattered that day: competing.

adrenaline comes with a number 2

I love to compete, and competing is about winning, the high you feel hitting the tape. Turning that final bend and seeing it at the end of the final straight. Looking back one last time to check that nobody is about to overtake you. Looking in front, closing your eyes and accelerating, feeling the spectators urging you on to victory, forgetting the pain, forgetting your body, being aware only of your mind, which is spinning with the emotions of the last seconds before you register how your stomach, dripping sweat, smashes the tape to the ground. It is the pent-up rage from the pressure lived over years, months, and the last hours of the race exploding in the final few yards, when you realize that all the sacrifice and effort have been worthwhile. It is what you feel for all those who have accompanied you in your career and contributed to this victory.

It is my mind that told me I could do it and now tells me I *have* done it. Everything comes together for those few seconds before I break the victory tape, and I feel a rush of amazing strength; I could run faster, leap higher and farther. But at the same time I feel weak with pure emotion, and I laugh, cry, and finally fall to the ground to kiss the earth. It brings goose bumps and tears of happiness. It is incredible. And it is what makes all the sacrifice worthwhile.

The taste of victory hooks you, addicts you like a drug, forces you to crave that feeling again, forces you to start back in on the process so that in a few months, or perhaps years, you can once again feel those moments of extraordinary strength and emotional fragility, moments of irrepressible happiness.

I have lost count of the weeks I have spent away from home, of the countries I have visited, and of the beds I have slept in. I began to compete 10 years ago, and it has been 10 years of seeking to relive again and again these emotions and sensations that take me to the peak of ecstasy and make me live life at a pace more suited to rock-and-roll musicians. Like a hard drug, it was enough at first to experience all of that two or three times a year, but my body could never get enough and each time demanded more and more insistently that I compete again. And so I finish one competition and immediately seek out another where I can get my next dose of pleasure. Road and bed. Week after week, day after day, I seek out new, ever-greater challenges to satisfy the needs of my body. Championships and world cups in Europe and Spain, prestigious races winter and summer, and in the weeks when there is no challenge in my diary, like an addict deprived of his fix, I scour magazines, the Web, and calendars for a race on the near horizon where I can satisfy my longing until it is time for the next important event on the schedule.

I'm sitting on the side of my bed, undressed and ready to sleep. The usual chaos from our get-togethers or the days before a race has vanished. Now my race kit is tidy: neatly folded white T-shirt with race bib already pinned on. Underneath, black pants. To their right, a pair of red-and-white socks, a windbreaker, the chip for my shoes, and my watch. A little farther to the right, next to the chair, three energy gels for the race, an isotonic drink for the warm-up, and my iPod with the list of songs all ready before the competition starts—16 songs especially selected and arranged to accompany me on my warm-up and help me go from a state of total relaxation to one of intense energy-burning activity. My spotlessly clean shoes on the floor. Jacket and pants to protect me from the cold in the morning while I go down to breakfast and wait to go out and warm up. All the rest—clothes, computer, the book I'm reading—is packed neatly in my bag so I won't be distracted in the morning. So my brain can concentrate solely on the race. As if my surroundings were an extension of my body and the neat orderliness of my surroundings was also vital for the orderliness I need in these hours before I fall asleep. My kit is all set.

I quickly review the course. I imagine I'm running. I imagine the path I'll find with each step and the pace I'll adopt at each point. I try to imagine the state of my body at every turn. I identify the exact place where I will take each gel, when I will drink water, and when I must accelerate or let the others set the pace. Everything is under control.

Following the advice Marco de Gasperi gave me last week about some of the Italian favorites running tomorrow, I imagine that they will kick off at an extremely fast rate in order to get a lead on the more marathon-style runners who will make up a lot of ground on me over the second, flatter half of the course. I should keep an eye on runners like Kuprizka, Ançay, and DeMatteis on the flat. Although if they ever do take the lead, I can always overtake them on the last downhill stretch. . . . Route reviewed, okay.

I get into bed and switch off the light.

"Have you seen the last film with . . . ?" asks my roommate.

"No. I don't think so. I read the book, but I don't think I've seen the film," I respond.

And we start two long parallel conversations: the one we can both hear, talking about books, girls, friends, anecdotes about other races, and the inner conversation with ourselves about the struggle that awaits us tomorrow, though no mention is made of gear, tactics, or rivals. This conversation addresses how we will deal with success or, above all, with failure if the race is a flop. How our egos and tempers will react and how the people around us will react.

We have spent all day imagining the feelings and emotions we will experience when we hit the tape, and that gives us the strength to want to win, and the inner conversation now focuses on the angst we will feel if we are beaten and our minds desperately look for an injury, an illness, a problem—an excuse not to experience that feeling of angst that makes us want to give up before we have even started.

The two conversations continue in parallel, come close, separate out, and try not to crack the façade that would reveal the fears that are raging in our minds.

The conversations come to an end. First the inner dialogue when it is plain there is no reason to give up before starting to fight or accept the failure we might face tomorrow, and when this conversation ends, the other fades away, of its own accord, as if it isn't interested in creating a wall to conceal our fears. Sleep begins to take possession of my body as I try to find the most comfortable position for sleep and healthy breathing, but although my eyes are shut, my head keeps spinning until finally sleep wins out.

It's gloomy and the sky is filled with clouds that don't seem at all threatening. I'm running down a path that winds through slopes hidden by thickets. The ground is dry, the track is covered in sand and stones, and the dry undergrowth alongside half smothers the gentle, undulating terrain. I look around me. I can't see a single mountain looming. The air is dry and arid, and I realize there's no breeze. All is silence, the kind of silence that is noisy and annoying, one you would like to break, but when you do shout, only a dry, distant sound emerges, as if it were disconnected from you. Gradually, as I run downhill, my legs seem heavier and stiffen to the point that I find it hard to continue. I don't understand—I'm going downhill; I should be able to run, should be able to accelerate. But my body doesn't react to the orders my brain sends out. It doesn't seem hot or cold, and an aid station appears. A girl and boy behind a table offer food and drink, but I can't make out what. I can't see their faces either. They stand there saying nothing as another runner runs up, fresh and smiling.

"Aleix!" I shout.

It can't possibly be Aleix, can it? He gave up competing years ago. What's he doing here? He doesn't reply, grabs something to eat, and keeps running downhill. I chase after him, forgetting how heavy my legs had felt. I start walking, until the heaviness and stiffness bring me to a halt. I fall down and drag myself along the track that is a mass of sand and stones. . . .

I get out of bed covered in sweat. The room is in darkness, and my friend is sleeping peacefully. All is quiet. However, this silence is warm, alive, and comforting and makes me feel secure. I look at the clock. It is midnight; we have been asleep for less than two hours. I try to breathe less frantically and to think of other things as sleep takes over again and brings no dreams.

I get out of bed six hours later, this time roused by the dull sound of the alarm. Gradually, we get up and switch on the light. Sleep flees the moment our brains register that the alarm signals three hours until the start of the race. There is no time to linger between the sheets. I quickly go downstairs and eat a slice of energy cake and 10 minutes afterward stretch out in bed once again, eyes shut, breathing regularly, while my heartbeat calms down. For the hundredth time over the last two days, I review the route for the race and my opponents. Everything is now in place; nothing can stop me.

An hour before the start, I jump out of bed, dress carefully, position the race bib so that it is perfectly straight, put the gels in my pocket, and tie my laces tight around the quick-lace so that my shoes perfectly fit the line of my feet and nothing can undo them. I head outside, and the music starts inside my head. Very loud sounds. Drums, vibrant electric rhythms that rise in volume and beat with each second. As if synchronized, my heartbeats begin to speed up. My brain tells me to jump, shout, and run as fast as I can. I take a couple of deep breaths and connect my iPod. I begin to run at a gentle pace, away from the other runners, in my own world. I am staring into the distance, far in front, visualizing the tape. A couple of sprints to wake my muscles up and get rid of the tension in my head and I am ready to go. I scrutinize the faces of the runners around me. I see serious faces, laughing faces, scared faces, and blank faces. I also see legs: hairless legs, muscular legs, white legs, and brown legs. Scary legs. Which legs will I see in the race? Because, given the effort I'll be making, I will find it hard to look up at faces, but I will see plenty of legs. I think I could recognize people by their legs rather than their faces after spending so many hours behind some runners. I am in my starting position, in the second row, not next to the fence or in the middle of the pack. The position I prefer. There is the odd laugh and comment, but you could cut the tension with a knife.

"One minute to go!" bawls the starter. Meanwhile, I start to feel the pressure from the group pushing forward, and the shoves start to come from all sides as people jostle to get in the best position possible. I don't think it is necessary to push now to gain a few inches. It's a long race that will put everyone in his place. Everyone is at the ready, bodies leaning forward, one leg in front, hand on watch, waiting to press the start button the moment the starting gun fires.

Time goes very slowly, almost stands still. Seconds seem like hours, and I find it harder and harder to follow the countdown because my thoughts can only focus on the actual start.

"Thirty seconds to go!"

Time doesn't race on but seems to stand still. As far as we are concerned, the world has come to a halt. People shout from behind the barriers, but I hear nothing. The silence is absolute, absorbed as I am by the tension of waiting for the starting pistol. My pulse races faster, ever more strongly. I feel every heartbeat in every part of my body, in my head, hands, legs. A countdown starts within me: 20, 19, 18, 17. . . . I feel my strength going, making me shake. My legs are stiff but wobbly and seem unable to bear my weight. . . . 10, 9, 8, 7 . . . I don't know if time has stopped altogether or if everything is speeding on uncontrollably. My legs are no longer shaking; my whole body now seems heavy and awkward. I'd find it hard to move my lips to shout. If nobody comes to support me, I will fall to the ground. . . . 3, 2, 1 . . . Suddenly, noise returns; I'm immersed in a world that is spinning fast, and I feel disoriented for a few seconds before my body responds powerfully and launches off. Now it is as light as a feather and able to move forward at great speed, nimbly avoiding the other runners in front of me until I take the lead.

The race develops as I had imagined it. At the outset, I accelerate for a couple of miles to break up the group so that no unknown competitor can set a gentle pace only to surprise me later, and also so that I can show off my own strength. I want to make it clear to the other runners that I am at my best and that today's race will be extremely tough. The first challenge is a sudden incline in a forest between tree roots and dark earth that takes us to 5,000 feet above sea level within very few miles.

A group immediately breaks away, and six of us are out in front. There is no unknown there; we are all among the favorites. I have already competed against two of these runners and hope they won't surprise me in any way. Helmut is now heading the group, and he has us all trailing breathlessly behind him. He is a tall Tyrolean runner with a very individual style whose strengths are ascents and long distances, though he is a man who loses ground to runners with more technique, such as myself, on short downhill runs. Robert is one of the best Czech runners, well trained as an athlete, a stately, well-balanced man who likes to take huge strides. He is a very dangerous runner in short races and over the flat. In fact, when we reach a flatter area on this first incline, he takes the lead in huge, explosive strides and rekindles the group. However, he always pays the consequences in longer races. I have never competed against the other three runners who make up the front group, but thanks to descriptions given by runners who have, I would say that I know them perfectly. The American is very strong in 5K races, is almost unstoppable on the flat, and for the moment seems to climb with great facility. Bruno is a young Italian runner, two years older than myself, who comes from cross-country, but he has always been outstanding in mountain races and achieved great results in short races and on steep courses. I don't think he will have any problems climbing, and being Italian, he will certainly run downhill like an arrow. The last runner in the group is Swiss with Portuguese roots: César has always been outstanding in races in Switzerland, and he has been in excellent form over recent months. He has recorded excellent times and won races ahead of runners as renowned as Tarcis. He is a good runner on any terrain, but prefers the flat and slopes that aren't so steep.

I feel good. It's a fast pace uphill, but I feel comfortable. Helmut has given way to Robert and César, who keep taking turns to fragment the small group in the lead, a tactic that soon bears fruit, as the American and Helmut start paying for the effort they have made over the first miles.

We reach the food stop at the top of the ascent, and I don't stop even for a breath but just grab a glass that a boy is balancing on his hand. I try to drink as I run, but what with the speed, jolts, and my fast breathing, I only manage a small gulp. The rest splashes onto my face and T-shirt. When we start on the flat, the pace settles down and we are four in the lead: Robert, Bruno, César, and myself. We've been running for over an hour, and I take a gel to give me the energy necessary to maintain that fast pace. I feel it slip down my throat, enter my body, and start distributing its sugar. However, simultaneously, I feel a lump in my stomach and want to vomit. My strength evaporates, and I feel queasy.

I am allergic to wasp stings, as I had discovered one day when I was stung by a wasp while cycling up the Passo dello Stelvio in the Dolomites. I couldn't remember ever being affected by a wasp sting. However, that sting had put me in the hospital within two hours. It happened a second time, just a day before this race, when I was coming back after lunch with the organizers and the rest of the runners. A wasp stung me on the thumb. If you aren't allergic, a sting hurts, but the pain goes away after a few hours and you can forget the sting. For me, on the other hand, it brings nausea, headaches, intense pain where I've been bitten, and an upset stomach for a whole day. If the sting had been on any other part of my body, like on my head or near an artery, I would have had hives everywhere and my tongue would have been swollen, with inevitable respiratory problems and blurred vision. So I had been lucky. I went to my bedroom and tightly bandaged my thumb to stop the poison spreading through my body.

I decided not to tell anyone and put it out of my mind until now, so as not to get discouraged and find concentration on the race ahead difficult. I need to think of a race as an enclosed space, a bubble. In this bubble only the race, the other runners, and myself exist. Everything else must be put aside. Excuses, lack of training, work, or romantic problems must be put aside. A race is a life that is born when you get up in the morning and dies when you cross the finish line.

And, obviously, I couldn't tell the other runners, since it would have been a weapon my opponents could have used against me right from the start, to strengthen themselves or to attack me at a moment of weakness. No, I have to show them I am perfectly in control, am not suffering, and am completely happy with the pace we have set. I have to show them that I am pleased with the way the race is going, that I am the one in charge and will be the one to decide who can take off in front or not. The one who will decide when it is time to make a sprint. I must make them believe they are fighting for second place.

Robert is putting the pressure on, and so is my stomach. I grit my teeth even harder, gulp in air, quicken my pace, and feel light. I reach his side and smile at him.

"Look at those beautiful peaks! This scenery is fantastic!" I say emphatically in one breath.

Without waiting for him to react, I pull back behind and breathe hard to take in air.

I gradually recover my strength, and with each step the need to hide my real state lessens. We have left the broad track and are now running along a gently undulating path that dodges the obstacles nature put in its way. It is a terrain that I enjoy, that allows me to run naturally and play with its whims. I haven't fully recovered my strength but decide to put the others runners to the test and see whether I can eliminate one or two opponents before we reach the final phase. I climb onto an incline and drive myself into the lead. Gathering speed with each descent, I sidestep trees and run swiftly up inclines. I soon see that no one is following me. Bruno is a few yards behind, and César and Robert seem out of it. As I feel comfortable on this terrain, I set a good pace and renew my energies for the last stage.

After a while I see three runners coming up very fast. The first to catch me is César, who stays with me whenever I quicken my pace to make it difficult for the other two to reach me. This is the final uphill stretch. The last 6 miles are a descent that seems like flat terrain until the final 2 miles to the finish, where it will be a short, sharp descent. It's a struggle to maintain this speed. The climb is hard, and I can feel César breathing down my neck. I decide to make one last effort to the next aid station, and from there I will decide what tactics to follow. I accelerate fast over the stones, scraping the ground with each step, but the breath of the runner behind me doesn't fall away. I don't want to turn around. I don't want to turn and show him that I'm finding it hard going, that I'm worried about where he is, about whether he is fresh or struggling.

We reach the Hotel Weisshorn food point, and I walk a few steps and grab a glass of water, which I drink without splashing it all over the ground. My throat is dry, and the cool water vanishes as if my mouth were a sponge. I grab another glass and break into a run. When I look up, I see César 100 yards in front. He didn't stop at the station, and Tarcis is coming up behind me after a spectacular run along the flat stretch. Robert is with him.

I focus on César. He is the one leading the race now, the one we have to catch, but our bodies don't seem to want to close in on each other. Tarcis and Robert are behind me, hoping I will be the one to drive them into the lead. I gradually get back into the race. It is the moment when I must decide whether I will do what my body is asking—slow down just a little, enough to remove the taste of blood from my mouth and get rid of the feeling that I might have a heart attack at any moment. After all, fourth place seems guaranteed, and a place on the podium may even come my way. I could be proud of that after the season I have had. But my brain tells me to ignore these signs and, in fact, defy them, and forces my heart to beat even more strongly and my legs to deal with more lactic acid. A radio commentary starts in my head. The broadcaster is describing the race, not the one now but the one that will start shortly:

> *César is running a fantastic final stage. Those chasing him are falling away, and it looks like nothing can come between him and victory. Hey, Kilian's fighting back! And putting so much energy into it! He's almost caught César. He's driving his body at an incredible pace. If he carries on at this rate, he will build a big lead. He has taken the lead and is maintaining an incredible pace. He's turned the last bend to the right and is now on the final straight. He's wonderful! He's about to seal a fantastic victory. The spectators are cheering. You can see tears of happiness in his eyes. . . .*

And as this commentary recedes, another takes pride of place in my mind. What will I feel when I am first past the finish line? I begin to imagine the future. I can already hear the spectators shouting. I can hear my name over the loudspeakers. I am ecstatic because I have succeeded. I did it. It is total bliss, a bliss I share with those who have helped me, and a great sense of relief and joy washes over me even as my body reacts with tears.

I suddenly start to shiver. These emotions are real. I feel my eyes moisten. The sensation is so strong that I want to feel it again. I'm craving it. I must catch César. I imagine I'm lassoing him with a long rope that I grab and pull on at each step so that I can close in on him; gradually, step by step, I do just that, until my shoes are right behind him, following in his footprints.

As I run behind César, I try to be aware of the posture my body is adopting. I try to run as straight-backed as possible so that I can breathe in the maximum amount of air and take big strides that drive my body on faster. I recall the words of Jordi, my trainer. Running is an art, he said, like painting a picture or composing a piece of music. And to create a work of art, you have to be clear about four basic concepts: technique, effort, talent, and inspiration. And all this must be combined in dynamic equilibrium. You must have perfect control of technique and avoid superfluous movements that don't help drive you forward and only waste energy. You must husband your movements, care for and protect them. Every runner has a natural way to run that he must follow and perfect. There are runners who take big strides and runners who prefer small steps. There are runners who run with their head erect and runners who stoop. There are runners who hold themselves in reserve and runners who attack from the very first. There is no way of running that can be imposed on everyone. There is no perfect way for every runner, but everybody has his perfect way of running. We discovered mine: It is running in step with nature, trying to communicate through my steps what nature is communicating to me. Not leaving a single trace on the terrain where I'm running, trying to be as silent as possible. Running as if I were floating over the path so that the earth hardly feels my feet brushing over its stones. Running and adapting to the terrain, taking small steps when running or big strides when walking up steep slopes, or trying to transform downhill stretches into a flowing dance between my body and the terrain. Never straining, but taking steps that flow naturally, as if they were an extension of that terrain.

From the day we first met, Jordi has always said that I have a gift for this sport, that my genetic makeup is perfect. But I've always been reserved and was never convinced that was true. I can remember the first ski event I won in an adult category. I was in my last year as a junior, and to reward my good results, the International Ski Federation took me to the European Cup. My eyes lit up when I saw that my idols—Florent, Manfred, Dennis—were there, and I could hardly believe it when I lined up next to them at the start.

The race started off at a very fast pace, and I was immediately left in no-man's-land between the trio of favorites who were 40 or 50 seconds in front and the group in pursuit that was a minute behind me. All of sudden, on the last climb, I joined the leading trio. *What's happened? Why have they stopped?* I wondered. *Why are they waiting for me?* I couldn't grasp the fact that I had caught up with them. I was completely at a loss for a few minutes. How could I possibly be with them? My body was numb. I couldn't stop thinking about how I was now running alongside my idols, the real people in those photos that filled my walls. When my mind started to function properly and I recognized the real competitive situation I was in, I didn't hesitate for a moment: I overtook them and went on the attack with all the energy I could muster. I continued to wonder, *Why don't they come after me? Why do they lag behind me?* I couldn't understand, but I pressed on to the finish line, where

I hugged the team selector, crying and jumping for joy, unable to believe that I had beaten Florent, the best Swiss runner, whom I partnered with years later in various races and who became the closest of friends.

However, as Picasso said, inspiration exists, but you have to work at it. Jordi and Maite always told me that talent and genetic makeup are useless without hard work. We must work constantly throughout our sporting lives, from the moment we wake up to the moment we go to sleep. No holidays or days of rest. It is the labor of an artisan, where artist and work are one and the same. It is work morning and afternoon, on leisure days, in good weather, and on trips to discover new valleys or to share training with friends. But there are also many days when the weather is bad, when you run in heavy rain, when it is cold or muddy, when your body is tired and you just want to stay in bed. When you get up and feel like staying warm inside, watching a movie and drinking tea, but you must go out and battle against wind and water. There are also many days of solitude, of more of the same, with only your iPod and a few wild animals that watch you from their dens for company as you run uphill and down.

We have been running in single file for some time, and no one wants to go on the attack. Tarcis takes the initiative and is leading the group at a very fast pace. I have positioned myself immediately behind him in order to react as quickly as I can if he decides to make a move. I have two cards to play: the first is to attack down the side where there are huge boulders and, using my technique, fire off 3 miles from the finish line, which would give me some margin to play with. The second is to start my attack later, on the last downhill slope, just under 2 miles from the line. While

I'm thinking about what might be the best strategy, Tarcis starts accelerating, making it increasingly hard to keep up the pace, and we start to fall a few yards behind. He speeds up and looks to be making his definitive spurt. He is leaving Robert and César behind. Perhaps now is the time for me to attack. . . . I look behind. They look as if they have accepted defeat. I am just about to change pace in order to pass Tarcis when he falls down in front of me. He had been taking too many chances on the descent, and his legs failed to keep up with his brain. I brake abruptly, look down, and give him my hand.

"Are you all right? Have you hurt yourself?" I ask.

"Shit! I'm fine, I'm fine," replies Tarcis, getting up.

As he does so, I hear those chasing us make a spurt. My first strategy is in tatters. I will have to wait for another opportunity to go on the attack. In the meantime, the four of us run together. I have few options left. We will reach the finish in just over 12 minutes, and though I am a runner who likes to control a race from the front and wait for the right moment to attack, I prefer to do that well before the finish in order to have more than one option if my opponents attack again. Now I will have to lay everything on a single card, and it will have to be the right one.

I feel Robert putting the pressure on behind me. I can feel his desire to overtake me. He has the strength to do so, and I don't have what I need to make a spurt myself. I must wait for the signal, for intuition to tell me now is the time and for my strength to flow back all at once.

Robert accelerates. I can't see or hear him, but I know he is making a move. I grit my teeth to finish a short climb and start downhill. Then I attack, speeding up and clearly stunning the others. As I pass, out of the corner of my eye I see Robert turn to look at those chasing him, and I register a tiny reaction that now becomes crucial: His eyes are no longer full of fire; they are small and have lost their brightness; the finish tape they want to smash through has vanished from their view. That tells me he is defeated, and I accelerate even more.

I never know when I will go on the attack. It is in that tenth of a second that the future of the race, victory or failure, will be decided. It is a moment you cannot plan; intuition must drive you to make a decision. An overconscious reaction will never come to good. If you attack too early, you will certainly pay for the excess effort, and if you leave it too late, you will lose. You have to make good use of the element of surprise. Find the key moment. This moment to change pace and go for the tape will always be the moment when the balance between self-confidence and doubt is shattered. You have to feel the fear that you can't do it in order to overcome it and launch into proving which of the two is right. And you must allow intuition to tell you when that moment has come, allow instinct to compel you forward, to tell you, "It's now or never." I'm a rational athlete; I enjoy analyzing races, planning them in advance, imagining how they will develop, dreaming them and rehearsing them in training, broadcasting them via imaginary commentators in my head. Sketching the outlines for the screenplay. I think I almost find writing that series of decisions in my head more satisfying than carrying them out for real, given that the screenplay we mark out is never respected, that there are always surprises. That is what makes competing so exciting, what makes it magical and turns it into an art—being able to follow the right impulse, knowing the one powering you into the lead is the right one, and keeping hold of it.

Life outside the race doesn't exist at such moments. The race is life, and it stops when you cross the finish line. An afterward doesn't exist; you can only think about getting there as quickly as possible. You don't think about the consequences the effort you are making might bring, the knocks or injuries awaiting you, because nothing else exists after the watch has stopped. Because the life we have created is at an end and we are left searching for a new one to create.

My legs can't stand the pressure; my breathing stops with each step, tries to minimize each impact. I'm not thinking about anything; my mind is blank. I only follow the sequence of emotions that I want to experience again. And as more come to mind, my legs accelerate and my heart beats faster. Seemingly out of control, my legs hurtle between rocks and undergrowth, but with each step they know exactly where they must go, where they must direct their strength. There are no feet, legs, or knees in reserve; there is no strength to retain. My body is at peak speed and my mind at the peak of concentration so as not to fall at every step.

I reach the asphalt, 100 yards, a bend to the right, and I look behind me. Nobody is in sight. And I have that feeling again.

But what does it mean to win? What is the real victory? When I cross the finish line, what is it that makes my hair stand on end or makes me feel that my feet are afloat, makes it so that I can't suppress the need to cry, makes me want both to run on and collapse to the ground? The real victory isn't the act of smashing through the tape and crossing the finish line; it's not seeing your name first on the list or standing on the highest step on the podium. This is not what makes your legs shake with fear and excitement. Victory, the real victory, is what is deep down inside each one of us. It's what we can't believe will ever happen despite all the training and will on our part, and yet it *is* what finally happens. Despite all the thinking and brandishing of calculators, after so many hours of preparation, after so many days of training, of telling ourselves that we can win—or simply finish the race—it is as if something in our unconscious is constantly telling us that it is impossible, that it would be too wonderful, too brilliant, too incredible for it to become reality. That what we want to achieve is only a dream. And when you cross the line, when you look behind and see that it is real, that you are flesh and blood, and that what seemed possible only in dreams has become real, you realize that *that* is the true victory.

Winning isn't about finishing in first place. It isn't about beating the others. It is about overcoming yourself. Overcoming your body, your limitations, and your fears. Winning means surpassing yourself and turning your dreams into reality. There have been many races in which I have finished first but haven't felt that I was the winner. I haven't cried when I crossed the line, haven't jumped for joy, and haven't been swept up in a whirlwind of emotions. I merely had to win the race, had to finish in front of the others, and before and during the race, I knew and was sure that I would finish first. I knew it was no dream and didn't think for one moment at any point what it would be like not to win. It was too easy, like a chef who opens his restaurant each day and knows exactly how all of his steaks will turn out. There's no challenge, no dream to wake up from. And as far as I am concerned, that isn't winning. On the contrary, I have seen big winners, individuals who have overcome themselves and have crossed the finish line in tears, their strength gone, but not from physical exhaustion—though that is also there—but because they have achieved what they thought was only the fruit of dreams. I have seen people sit on the ground after crossing the finish line of the Ultra-Trail du Mont-Blanc, and sit there for hours with blank looks, smiling broadly to themselves, still not believing that what they have achieved isn't a hallucination. Fully aware that when they wake up, they will be able to say that they did it, that they succeeded, that they vanquished their fears and transformed their dreams into something real. I have seen individuals who, though they have come in after the leaders have had time to shower, eat lunch, and even take a good siesta, feel that they are the winners. They wouldn't change that feeling for anything in the world. And I envy them, because, in essence, isn't this a part of why we run? To find out whether we can overcome our fears, that the tape we smash when we cross the line isn't only the one the volunteers are holding, but also the one we have set in our minds? Isn't victory being able to push our bodies and minds to their limits and, in doing so, discovering that they have led us to find ourselves anew and to create new dreams?

it's not only about competing | 3

Night begins to fall at my back, the sun sinking behind sharp peaks and snow-swept walls of rock, offering up its last shards of light to tinge the sky red to match the autumnal leaves. Following the rhythm of my steps, the brightness in the west gradually begins to disappear as the mantle of darkness covers the sky, hiding the daytime oranges and greens of the woods, which take on darker, duller, rawer hues. The track begins to vanish beneath my feet, and I find it hard not to stumble on the stones that stick up. The heat vanishes along with the light; the temperature drops, and my cheeks starts to freeze in the icy air, as does my nose. The pupils in my eyes dilate as much as they can to anticipate what the soles of my feet will be feeling. In those first minutes in the dark, my steps are clumsy and I fall to the ground when I trip over a tree root that straddles the track. However, my eyes gradually adapt to the darkness, and as sight gives way to the senses of touch and hearing, I can see as if it were daylight. Today, for the first time, I am tired. For the first time in many days, my eyes feel heavy and my mind sinks into a world of heavy darkness. I remember this feeling. It's a memory from a few years ago, when I was running along the paths of the Tahoe Rim Trail.

You don't need to compete to be able to feel the intense emotions of finishing, the excitement of crashing through the finish line tape. You can feel that same boundless happiness even if you eliminate the highs of the cheering spectators, beating other runners, the flashes and spotlights of photographers or television cameras. It is a happiness you alone feel as you experience that strength powering you to succeed. It is a deeply internal happiness, without the rage that comes with racing, a calm, soothing happiness that transports you to a world of total peace, where time and space come to a halt and you feel that your body and your soul are completely, blissfully at rest.

I hear footsteps running this way and that along the black wooden balcony that spans all the rooms in this American hotel where we are staying. I turn over in bed and stretch my hand out to the clock on the bedside table. It is 4:25 a.m. The alarm won't go off for five more minutes, and even though I don't feel at all sleepy, I turn over, wrap the blankets around me again, and shut my eyes. Outside, the footsteps sound faster and faster and the whispers louder and louder. I put my head under the blanket and press myself down into the soft mattress. I notice the heat running through my body, from my toes to my cheeks, and feel almost as if I were lying by a fireside. I also feel my arms, legs, and torso move subtly, seeking the best position, one I could enjoy for hours. My muscles are completely relaxed. My mind feels at peace in a silence that is broken only by the footsteps and whispers outside my window. I could spend hours, even days, like this, not moving a single finger, with my body and mind completely at ease, not having to worry about anything. My body doesn't exist for the moment; it doesn't bother me or hassle me; it doesn't provoke cold or heat; it doesn't prompt pain or require any effort. For the moment my mind is alone, its links to the earth severed; for the moment I can enjoy my thoughts and let my dreams give me a body that can fly. When it comes to separating body from mind and being able to fly free, isn't a good bed much more practical than those 165 miles waiting for me outside?

I am seduced by these ideas as the heat and tranquility afforded by my comfortable bed contrast with the excitement mounting on the other side of my bedroom walls. What if I have already resolved the search I took on to test myself and find happiness? Have I traveled into the mountains of California's Sierra Nevada, to run the Tahoe Rim Trail in record time, only to understand that a good bed was the solution in life?

I burst out laughing. I was on the brink of letting my thoughts trick and persuade me, but that isn't happiness; it's the comfort zone! With that thought, I jump out of bed and switch on the light and the radio. I get pineapple juice out of the freezer and heat up a slice of energy cake. While it's heating up, I take off my pajamas and put on the clothes that will probably stay on me for the next two days and nights. Socks, shoes, leggings, thermal shirt, polar lining, hat, and watch. I look at the time: 4:45 a.m., five minutes left before I have to head to the start of the race. Even though this isn't an organized race, and in the end *I* decide the starting time, we had settled on 5 a.m. so that the support team would be able to predict the times when I would pass by each point on the route, though even then only approximately, because when a route lasts a good 40 hours, it is hard to anticipate exactly when you will reach any one particular point. I quickly devour the slice of energy cake, grab the GPS and a few snack bars and gels that I'll take for the first few hours, and switch off the light. Before I leave, I grab another piece of energy cake. I'll need it.

Swallowing the last crumbs, I head toward the start. It's still dark. It's 4:55 a.m. when I reach the bridge over the Truckee River in Tahoe City. The 165-mile Tahoe Rim Trail is a circuit around Lake Tahoe, though not around the lakeside; it passes through the mountains that surround the lake, with severe dips and peaks. I had been looking at those dips and peaks and decided I wanted to get the worst over on the first day, noting that Tim Twietmeyer, who holds the record of 46 hours, decided to make this his point of departure. I, too, thought it was a good spot. But I am questioning the decision to leave at 5 a.m. If this were a race lasting 15 or 16 hours, a 5 a.m. start would be quite obvious, since that way we could take advantage of every hour of daylight and run the least amount of time at night. However, if it were a cross-country trail lasting some 20 hours, it would make more sense to leave at night in order to run the first hours in the dark, when the body is fresher, and then to run most of the course under the heat of the sun and finish with the last light of day. If it were a route taking in the range of 30 hours, it would make sense to leave at dawn, since that way we would run only one night and two days. However, today, at 5 a.m., still in the pitch-dark and in freezing cold temperatures, I don't understand why we must leave so early if I will have to spend two nights and two days running. Really, you can make whatever combination you like: day-night-day-night, night-day-night-day. I could even start at midday, after lunch, because I'd still have to run for two nights and two days.

To cries of encouragement from my pacers and support team, I take my first steps northward at 5 a.m. There are 20 or so of us participating in this adventure, each with a specific role to play. However individual a sport may be, however many hours I run without seeing anyone, and however many miles I need to cover, sport and life are always about teamwork, in which each person contributes their grain of sand to help the adventure reach a successful outcome. I've given my legs the desire to fight with all the strength I can muster. Sònia is a doctor and has brought her knowledge and expertise to cure any injury and, above all, to give me moral support at the most grueling moments. Olivier and Benjamin have studied the route, which each now knows like the back of his hand, and will be at different points to give me food and drink. Gino and Jean Yves are the representatives of the brand that's sponsoring me and have come to help wherever necessary: in the kitchen, on the mountain, transporting my pacers. The pacers are Adam, Josh, Ross, Sean, Kevin, Jean-mi, and Bryon, who by turn will accompany me over the whole course. The film crew comprises Marlène, Raf, O. J., Mimo, and Lolo. Finally, Lotta is responsible for the overall organization, although everyone in fact does a bit of everything—cooks, gives out food, lends mutual encouragement, gets my clothes ready, and gives me support. And no one sleeps.

Bryon and I start running. I feel fresh and light. My feet feel nimble, finding the quickest path and powering me into the woods of California. I can hear Bryon start to pant behind me, and that motivates me as the first light of day begins to shine through the trees. A spectacle of nature unfolds before us.

The sun shines brightly between the tall pines north of the lake on the high plain of California. The light has a strength, is intense, solid, with a body of its own. It is no mere spectator illuminating nature, but is transformed into a living element, like the mountains, lake, or the sky itself. The show of colors offered by the combination of water and light relegates to second place the baroque architecture traced by the old pine woods between the small lakes and undulating terrain. The sinuous shapes seem designed by the best modernist architects, their impossible knots like gargoyles on Renaissance cathedrals and their thick, striated bark giving the forest the massive presence of a Romanesque monastery. Green phosphorescent lichens bring light to spaces not bathed by the sunbeams that are painting the tree bark and sand red.

In this dance of colors we are also like dancers striding forward, possessed by their energy, and we tease the broad path that glides between gentle undulations and then amuses itself by changing rhythm with each bend, each descent, and each sunbeam that passes us by. I spur my legs on and feel my muscles tensing before I drive them harder and then relax completely as my legs glide through the air. My watch records a pace of about 10 miles an hour. I feel really good, and it's as if my feet prefer not to make contact with the ground. We swerve through the trees at top speed, flying on silent strides, breathing in the fresh air, alert to everything around us.

I feel as if I have been transported back in time, like a young Indian brave silently pursuing an elk that is running away, hiding among the huge trees. I must move swiftly forward, follow the majestic animal's elegant strides, but I must also advance silently, almost without touching the ground, so that I don't trample on a branch and give away my position. As I peer between the branches of the huge, lichen-covered pines, I feel the strength of the warriors who ran along these slopes a few centuries ago. I smell their scent in the moss, I see their shadows running by my side between the rocks we are crossing, and I see their faces reflected in the rivers where I stop and drink the water they once drank. I hear their words on the wind that caresses our faces as we leave the woods. And I turn myself into one more member of their tribe as I run along the same tracks where they ran, lit by the same light they saw come to life and die.

Today we are left with what was strongest, with what men were unable to destroy. We are left with rocks, rivers, sand, and trees. Tremendous efforts have been made to conserve these natural spaces and, unlike many areas on the planet that have suffered wholesale destruction, these parks preserve nature almost as wild as the nature experienced by the indigenous tribes. Away from the few paths that cross the park, animals live peacefully, far from the dangers represented by modern man, where nature can breathe and reproduce without being choked by clouds of smog from big cities. Hundreds of acres enjoy a cycle of existence imposed by the passage of time and confront only the aggression of snow in winter, rain in spring, and heat in summer. However, just 60 miles to the west, trees have disappeared and animals die trying to cross the labyrinths of asphalt where a world circulates that is alien to the forces of nature, where rock has ceased to be what is hardest, where water no longer flows along the bottom of valleys, and where food isn't under the ground, doesn't hang from a tree, or doesn't lie hidden in a den, but is wrapped in plastic and displayed on supermarket shelves.

Nature has been trapped in islands surrounded by a sea of fakery and artifice, where people can contemplate its wonders and take photos with its inhabitants, be they animals, plants, trees, rocks, rivers, or mountains, as if they were strange exhibits in a museum, never understanding that in times past, those rocks, valleys, and rivers were not a heritage that had to be protected, but were our homes, our supermarkets, our schools.

Immersed in this spectacle of nature, we have run more than 37 miles almost without noticing and have left the northern side of the lake behind us. The sight of the highest peaks and the best possible views over the lake have been a real tonic as they enabled me to see the entire route for the first time—and it doesn't seem that long. I've already run a fifth of the way, and the prospect of repeating four more times what I have already done doesn't strike me as so difficult.

Six hours in, the sun has taken possession of the sky and I'm beginning to feel hungry. The moment I reach Tahoe Meadows, I down a small plate of macaroni dressed with oil and salt before starting on the second part of the route through the mountains on the east side of the lake.

The track continues its monotonous alternation of gentle dips and ascents, never steep enough to force me to walk or so stony that I must consider the best way to place my feet to clear the hurdles. The passage of time has brought with it fatigue and an end to the feeling of light legs that never touch the ground and eager eyes that catch every small movement around me. I still feel well and strong, but the first signs that this strength will end sooner rather than later are starting to show. Big driving strides have given way to steps close to the ground to avoid wasting energy. My gaze is only focused on the stretch of path in front of me, distancing me from the surrounding landscapes and my roaming thoughts of the past. I start to wonder why I was so stupid to have wasted so much precious energy at the start. My average speed was very high, and my running, along with my instincts and heart, is beginning to suffer the consequences. I still have a long way to go, and even though I'm not losing pace, I anticipate that I will soon. I try to ignore these thoughts and conceal them from my pacers and from myself by engaging in animated debate with Adam and Kevin and playing games with the wind that has picked up as the day has progressed.

Yet again my feet sink into the sand on the path, but I force myself to keep running and puffing. When I look up from the ground, I see we are running between two lakes. To our right, a half mile downhill, is the eastern shore of Lake Tahoe, and to the left, a large lake spreads out and follows the path for hundreds of yards. I smile when I see this beautiful spectacle, but I don't want to expend energy talking about how pleased I am to be running in such scenery. So we follow the route in silence, with Kevin behind me. We are running along a broad ridge into a strong headwind that makes each step more difficult, as if the 120 pounds I weigh have suddenly become 150. I try lowering my head and holding my hands close to the sides of my body to give myself more aerodynamic lines. I manage a few hundred yards like that, but lack of air forces me to look up and take in deeper breaths. When I do that, I realize that the path is imperturbably following its familiar pattern. *Blasted paths,* I think. *Couldn't they have made more direct tracks rather than ones going twenty times round the mountain to get to the top?*

The sun is starting to shine gently on the mountains to the west, and so far there hasn't been a single ascent that has forced me to walk. I want to find a steep ascent I have to walk up or climb. I want to encounter a tricky descent, a slope that makes me watch where I put my feet so that I don't fall, when running becomes a dance over rocky hurdles and not a simple succession of skimming steps that take me forward. As I think these thoughts, I see Olivier's silhouette at the top of this ascent. It doesn't seem too far off and I need a stop, not to eat but to break out of the dragging rhythm I have gotten into. I look down and accelerate to reach the stop quickly. I count to 100 and, panting, look up again, hoping to see Olivier in front of me. However, he is still a long way off; I would even say he is farther away. I don't seem to be making any progress, and every step seems to defy my expectations. Finally, however, we reach the hill where Olivier is waiting and I sit on the ground. I take a gel and briefly gaze at the two lakes we have left behind. Losing no time at all, I start running again. I have to reach

Kingsbury South before nightfall, and the sun is rapidly beginning to go down behind the mountains on the other side of the lake.

My steps echo monotonously along the track. I finally reach the mountain ski station of Kingsbury along with the last embers of daylight, and I stop for 40 minutes to eat, rest—physically and mentally—and gather strength for the second part of the course. I have run some 75 miles, but have yet to reach halfway. The dry, earthy terrain has covered my body in dust, and I have dirt in my shoes and socks, which has given me huge blisters that have begun to hurt now that I have stopped. As I eat a large plateful of gnocchi, Lotta washes my feet in cold water and Sònia prepares a syringe of Betadine to clear the liquid from the blisters.

"It will just sting slightly," she says when she sees the fear in my eyes as she brings the syringe close to my feet.

"All right," I reply halfheartedly. I know it's the only solution if I am to continue for another 90 miles without being forced to wear bigger shoes.

She sticks a needle into the blister and takes the liquid out before injecting Betadine.

"Ahhh!" I moan. It feels like my foot has just been stuck inside a pan of boiling water. I quickly take my foot away from Sònia and blow hard on the blister.

"I told you it would only hurt a little bit, because I didn't want to frighten you. Come on, that's one less," Sònia says persuasively. She gradually burns the skin off the blisters until my feet don't hurt anymore; whether it is because the blisters have been eliminated or because the burning process has left me totally numb to pain, I do not know.

The cold returns with a vengeance as soon as the sun disappears, and I wrap up for the night: long-sleeve T-shirt, windbreaker, gloves, and hat. Ross, a strong runner who lives and runs here, will accompany me on the first part of the night, as the paths are not clear and apparently it is very easy to take a wrong turn. It is a weight off my mind to run next to someone who knows the area so well. We are ready to go: clothes on, last gnocchi eaten. I make sure my headlamp has batteries, do stretches to loosen up legs that have started to feel the miles, and once again we run off in the dark to shouts of encouragement from the team, though this time at quite a different pace. We gradually climb the track that zigzags across the Kingsbury ski slopes. Our gentle pace warms my legs, and my joints relax and expand as we make headway. My strength returns, and I feel better and better as we run up between fields and woods. It is a cold night that reminds me of my winter training long ago, when we would return from high school and go for runs in the dark over Montellà. The wind biting my face activates my senses and gives me energy to run strongly once we leave the wooded areas around the ski slopes and move into a wild territory of lakes and craggy peaks. A hard climb up a sandy track takes us up to East Peak, where an extraordinary nighttime vista of the southern part of Lake Tahoe extends before us.

In order to maintain the pace and at the same time disconnect and think of things other than running, the route, and what I should eat, I let my mind imagine instead the adventures we might have. I imagine we are escapees from prison, in flight and hiding in these woods. Or that we are Indian braves in pursuit of a herd of deer or carrying an urgent message to a neighboring tribe.

Running has turned into a chore, like breathing, eating, or going to the bathroom (which here means going behind a pine tree, a rock, or, when your strength fails you and you can't wander far from the path, under a rock only a few inches away). I decide to think about what I need to do next week: I have to buy a present for Maria because it's her birthday on Wednesday, I have to phone the mechanic and arrange for the car to have its 50,000-mile checkup, and I need to go to the supermarket when I get home because the freezer is empty.

Sometimes I stop thinking altogether and simply let myself be carried along by the rhythm of a song, singing loudly. This is one of the best ways I have found to distract myself and forget about time so that the hours pass more quickly. The only problem, on this occasion, is that I have left my iPod at home and I don't know if it is exhaustion or if what they say about running destroying neurons is true, but songs start to stick, become etched in my mind, and, however much I want to press the button and go on to the next song, I can find no way to stop myself from repeating the same song, time and again. During a 3- or 4-hour race or, stretching it, a 6- or 7-hour competition, this is tolerable, but it is a problem if the song gets stuck a few hours after the start and you've been at it for almost 20. Imagine the state my nerves are in after repeating thousands of times, *"Oooh life . . . is bigger . . . is bigger and . . . na na na na na . . . Losing my religion!"* Without the help of the iPod, I can remember only this refrain, and I have been trying to remember how the hell the rest goes for the last 20 hours. Although I'm at my wit's end, 2 or 3 hours go by almost without my noticing while I hunt for those lyrics, and in that time I forget my tired legs, the cold, and the fact that there are still so many miles to go.

However, inevitably, as the miles go by, the monotony sets in again. As we leave the ridges behind and run back into the thick woods, the wind disappears and takes with it my alert senses. My legs still feel light, and my heart wants to carry on the struggle, but my senses feel numbed as we make the descent from Thompson Peak. I abandoned the sense of touch hours ago so as not to feel the pain in my legs and the blisters on my feet. The next sense to disconnect is my hearing, which blots out the sounds of the forest and whatever Ross is saying. Sight soon follows: My eyes nearly shut, to the point that my lashes are so close I cannot make out the terrain and I begin nodding off. I burst into loud song and jump as I run in order to try to reactivate my senses. A few paces behind me, Ross probably thinks I've gone crazy, but it helps wake me up, warding off drowsiness. I run powerfully for a few minutes, but the many hours of running soon hit me, and my eyelids begin to feel heavy again as my rhythm becomes more monotonous. I struggle against this deadweight and start singing again, even more loudly this time, and I accelerate around bends, leap over stones, and grab hold of trees to gather speed and adrenaline and activate the hormones that should be keeping me awake.

Despite all this, a few minutes later my eyes shut once again, this time with a vengeance, and I give up the struggle, letting the weight of my lids seal in sleep. A state of well-being spreads through my body, and my agitation disappears, as does exhaustion. Pain recedes and my thoughts evaporate. I forget my body, letting myself be carried away by a world where everything is easy. Suddenly, my thoughts jolt me back to the real world. *Was I running? I don't remember stopping. . . . Am I still running?* I open my eyes in a panic. *Where am I?* I look to both sides of me. I have drifted a good 100 yards away from the path and am sitting on the ground between pine branches and huge anthills. Very few seconds can have passed, because Ross is still coming behind me along the path. I walk back, thinking *I cannot go on like this*. I know I ought to stop for a while to sleep, at least long enough to get rid of this drowsiness so that I can finish the run. I remember hearing someone say that they napped for half an hour to shake off drowsiness and were then able to continue for a few more hours. Yes, I will try that. It is only 6 or 7 miles to Big Meadow, where my team is waiting and where I decide I will stop and sleep.

After a hard hour's running while trying to stop my eyes from shutting again, we finally reach the road to the south of the lake. I quickly stretch out on the hard surface of the car park with a sleeping bag over me. I fall asleep immediately. I don't have time to think how cold and hard the ground is, whether I am on my back or my front. I simply fall into a deep sleep.

"Kilian!" I hear an echo deep in my dreams. "It's time. Kilian!" Each time it sounds louder and clearer. "Kilian!"

I open my eyes and see a light above my head. I gradually wake up and recognize Sònia on the other side of the headlamp.

"Is it late?" I ask as I rub my eyes. I still feel dead. My drowsiness has only slightly receded, and weariness seems to pin me to the ground. *It can't be,* I tell myself. *I've got more than 65 miles to cover. It can't be.* I sit up and knock myself on the head several times to wake myself up and prepare to get up and continue running. But my legs don't respond. They fold under me, and I can't tighten my muscles and pull myself up. I make a second attempt. It's not simply that they don't respond; when I try, I feel a stabbing pain in every muscle in my body. I think, *My God! If I feel like this when I try to get up, what on earth am I going to feel on the last 65 miles of the run?* With great difficulty, I pull myself up like a clumsy doll with wooden legs. That is when I realize that the temperature has dropped dramatically; I had been sleeping too soundly for it to register. I drink a hot cup of tea, and after an energetic stretch that makes my joints crack and pop, I start running south accompanied by Sean. It's still five hours to sunup.

As always after I've made a stop, my legs slowly begin to warm up and I feel well again, leaving my gripes behind me. I begin to settle into a good stride and try to accelerate to make up for the time I've wasted sleeping. I'm not sure how my body will react over the final section, and I want to set a good pace just in case. I debate with Sean, the run is pleasant and easy, and I feel my feet have rediscovered the air and lightness they lost. We follow the path that slopes gently uphill in lengthy, straight stretches through a dense pinewood. We reach the top of a hill and start on an equally gentle descent. I know we should be turning northward soon, but the path continues south. I have just begun to worry when a lake suddenly appears in front of us. *Where the hell did this lake come from?* I wonder as I continue to try to work out where we are. I try to catch a glimpse of the outline of the mountains, but can see nothing clearly between the pitch-black of night and the thick clouds. It's obvious to me that we shouldn't have come to this lake, but where then is the right track? I review the path we have followed from Big Meadow: We had taken the only path there was, climbed for a small distance, and when we reached the flat, turned left at the crossroads. Shit! We should have gone right. We've run 4 miles since that wrong turn, and the thought that we now have an extra 4 to do is hardly exhilarating, but in the pitch-dark and not knowing exactly where we've landed, we have no choice. And, in any case, didn't I come here to test out what my body is capable of? How far it can go? I've come to the heart of the West to find out what my body and mind can do. Am I now going to lose heart over a mere 8 extra miles? On the contrary, I turn around, smile broadly at Sean, and say, "Sean, more miles, more fun!" He bursts out laughing, and we begin to retrace our steps, still laughing. The excitement or rage at taking a wrong turn and having to make up the time we've spent discovering unexpected landscapes wakes me up all of a sudden; my senses are firing at 100 percent again. This excitement gives me an energy boost that allows us to make the backtrack in half an hour, singing, laughing, and swapping stories. We return to the crossroads and this time take the path on the right, turning into a gentle climb through woods to an area of alpine meadows.

Our excitement gradually subsides, and our strength begins to abandon us as well. Not only our strength; the battery in my head-lamp is running out, as if it were a metaphor for my state of mind, and a few minutes later, Sean's gives out as well. It must be 10 or 12 miles to Echo Lake, where the team is waiting with new batteries, though probably by the time we get there, the light of day will have resolved that little setback for us.

Running in the dark isn't unpleasant; on the contrary, it keeps you awake, activates your senses, and puts your whole body on the alert. Your senses work toward a common aim: to avoid falling down or colliding with a tree. I recall our outings in the dark when I was a child and try to achieve maximum concentration. I dance around the shadows on the ground, react playfully with my feet and balance. I accelerate and feel my feet adapt to the ground, touching and exploring as my body attempts to keep balance by juggling with my hands and arms. I like this kind of game, where I feel I'm about to drop but manage to keep upright at the last minute by swaying a hip or grabbing at the air. This is exactly what I had hoped to do on this adventure: Take my body to the limit of its strength and resistance, and train my mind to withstand pain. I'm attempting to climb to the very tip of the blade of the sword without falling off the other side, and I think I'm succeeding.

A few hours later we reach the bottom of the valley at Echo Summit, a broad, open track in the first light of day. I have been running for more than 24 hours and am pleased that my body has stood the test so far, apart from pain in my thigh muscles, tendons, and hamstrings; soreness in my hip and knee joints; a few blisters on my feet; fatigue; cold; and slight stabbing pains in my knees. Apart from all that, I feel wonderful, that I still have reserves of inner energy and strength left to draw on. I can feel that my muscles, though hurting, are holding up well. My head stays calm and focused, and I know my body can still accelerate if I put my mind to it.

As we reach Echo Lake, daylight reveals a complete change in the weather. Threatening clouds are gathering over the mountains on the other side of the lake, exactly in the direction we now have to run. After resting and drinking steaming hot tea in which we dunk cookies and slices of energy cake, Jean-mi and I get ready to take on the longest section of the course without any support: across 31 miles of the Desolation Wilderness. It is a stony terrain, with huge slabs of granite that cross the countless lakes of Aloha and Velma. In the soft light beneath those dark clouds, it is as if we were walking across a planet where no life exists, where we are the only people left alive after a nuclear explosion and are trying to find other living beings in a vast desert. Or perhaps my eyes can no longer distinguish between the reality they see and what goes on inside my head. Monotony has taken ahold again, and exhaustion, after more than 125 miles, feels very different. Now, fatigue isn't pain in my legs, isn't stabbing pain in my knees, isn't about drowsiness or breathing. Instead, everything has come to a halt. Everything. I am empty, my legs have lost their strength, I can't move my arms, and my body can't accelerate uphill. I'm breathing through my nose, with my mouth shut. I don't have the strength to send very much oxygen to my lungs; my diaphragm can't contract and distribute it. My feet drag. Above all, my head is empty and my gaze aimless. I don't feel the usual elation, or even react at all, as I contemplate the splendid views over Lake Tahoe and the spectacular crags of Jacks Peak. I can't keep up a conversation. Words spoken by my companion and even the sounds of nature all echo in the far distance. Snowflakes start falling, but I don't feel the cold; I can't even feel the pain that only hours ago was torturing me. And thought has vanished from my mind. I can't summon a song to help keep my rhythm; I don't have the strength to remember a single one. I can't think how many minutes it will take to reach the next hill I have to cross. I have lost the notion of space. I can't imagine the future, the finish line. The future doesn't exist in this void of mine. I can't daydream, can't even wonder what I'm doing here, why I've come and why I've chosen this accursed sport. Memories, thoughts, and dreams have faded; there is only a void in my head. Everything has disappeared, and I'm moving forward like a robot, not knowing what my destiny is, not knowing what to expect. Inertia keeps my legs running; my heartbeat and breathing continue to work without a conscious will to drive them on.

Time passes; the snow passes; rocks, valleys, peaks, lakes, meadows, clouds pass. The sun crosses the sky from east to west, but time has come to a stop as far as I'm concerned. None of that exists, nothing is real, and nothing is imaginary. My spirit seems to have disappeared, and my body merely follows the impulses for which it is programmed. I hear voices disturbing the void within me. But there is nobody around for many miles. I look behind, look at the peaks, then immediately conclude it must have been the wind, rustling leaves and tricking me into believing I am at the end of this stretch, where all the team will be waiting.

Or maybe I have started to hallucinate. Colleagues who have run the Ultra-Trail du Mont-Blanc or the Diagonale des Fous and have been running for more than one night have told me that sometimes on the second day, chairs appear in the middle of the track, and as they take a seat to rest, they fall on the ground as the chair vanishes. Or that trees come to life on the second night and attack them with branches. No, I haven't had a hallucination. *I should be so lucky*, I think, *because then I'd have something to fill this void.*

Emptiness. A step, a snowflake. Another step, wind, yellow grass. Sand, another step. White, 33 hours, another step. These are my thoughts over the last six or seven hours. I try to think in monosyllables so as not to waste the energy necessary to connect two neurons.

A field of yellow ears of corn on top of sand extends in front of me. The wind sways the corn, and though the sun has swept away the clouds and the snow, it has not warmed the air. Figures are visible in the distance among the undulating gold, and sound starts to return. I look at the ground, at the sand, and look up again to see whether the figures are in the same place. Now they're not only appearing between the ears of corn, but are also swaying and waving their arms. I realize that they are not hallucinations: I have reached Barker Pass, where my support team is waiting. My mind reacts, driven by a desire to run toward them, but my body remains impervious to the orders issued by my mind. Finally, I just sit on a stone, and Lotta brings me sandwiches, tea, and cookies. I'm not hungry. My stomach has shrunk and lacks the strength to digest anything it might be given. I feel totally powerless. I'm not the one dictating my movements. Where has my spirit gone? Where is my strength? I close my eyes, which are looking aimlessly at the horizon. No, I tell myself, I can't have gotten this far, can't have run 156 miles only to throw in the towel on the last 17 miles. No, I have not reached my limit yet. With a renewed sense of purpose, I open my eyes and look toward Tahoe City, on the other side of the peaks looming before me. I force myself to eat a couple of cookies soaked in tea, knock the dust off my shoes yet again, and for the first time in many hours a smile spreads across my face.

I stand opposite the trail and shut my eyes once more. I can feel the cold, and the wind riffles my hair and clothes. I choose a song, one of my favorites, one of those that when you hear it, your hair stands on end and your heart speeds up with the beat. In my head, I can hear how the bass begins at a gentle pace—*toom-toom*—and the drums riff, underlining the rhythm. I see the stage in the dark, the musicians in the center, heads bowed, listening to the bass resonating into the distance. It gets louder and louder until, at the moment of climax, I imagine the stage suddenly lighting up and the singer and the electric guitar joining in an explosion of rhythm. The sound is true and fresh. The mountains loom where the stage was, and clear and precise, like the singer's voice, a path opens up between the mountains.

I feel fresh and light now, without the heaviness I had accumulated over the last 156 miles. I turn and burst into a run, not touching the ground, disappearing at top speed between the mountains to the beat of that electric music. I open my eyes wide and feel a wave of strength surge up from my feet to my hair. I run strong, at a pace my legs have not enjoyed since yesterday. It's not that all the pain has disappeared. It is there, and makes itself felt, but rather than stealing the focus of my attention, it is now tucked away in a corner of my mind. So what is it that makes me feel lighter? My tiredness is even greater than before; my legs feel heavier and are straining more. Then why, despite tiredness, can they run so quickly? What has changed in my body? Absolutely nothing. But one small thing has changed in my consciousness: I now know I can do it and can see the finish line at the end of the path. It is within my grasp; I can already touch it and feel it.

Running the last few miles, surrounded by the whole team here to accompany me and make this dream come true, I realize finally that the threshold isn't in my body or in my legs. I see now that I could have gone faster along the whole course; I could have gone at the speed I'm traveling now. Why had I put on the brakes? It was my mind. My mind had led me to lose concentration and motivation, had placed difficulties and obstacles in my path and blurred the image of the finish line, disorienting me and making me lose sight of my goal and my determination to get there, made me think it wasn't possible. But I'm not disappointed. On the contrary, I've made a great discovery: Thresholds don't exist in terms of our bodies. Our speed and strength depend on our body, but the real thresholds, those that make us give up or continue the struggle, those that enable us to fulfill our dreams, depend not on our bodies but on our minds and the hunger we feel to turn dreams into reality.

As the path ceases to wind between the trees and flattens out to follow the course of the river, the clock strikes 7 p.m. Finally, I can let myself go. There is no limit, the pain has gone, and my legs have recovered their full range of motion. Strength has come back to my lungs and heart. As if it has returned to the starting point, my body erases everything it has suffered since I set out and regains the sensations felt 38 hours ago, the same strength I started with, the same motivation. In the last few hundred yards before I close the circle, the pain and heaviness of all the miles I have run disappear. I don't need to hold anything in reserve or take precautions. I break into a sprint, jump a barrier in the middle of the trail rather than go around it, and shout as floodlights illuminate the finish line. I look at the ground and can't hold back my tears. Images rush into my head of everything I have experienced over the last couple of days—the light from the dawning sun, the lakes, trees, heat, cold, snow, waste, sorrow, and happiness. Right now I don't feel proud of myself, of what I have achieved, of the fact that I have shared in this physical and emotional adventure; all of that will come later, when the tears are done and I can analyze more coolly what I have accomplished. Now I can only let pure emotion flow, emotion from seeing that I was able to achieve what I had set out to do, despite the difficulties and suffering. I can't begin to describe this emotion; it is like taking a firm grasp on happiness, ecstasy, and joy and raising them to the power of infinity. It is as if my body and mind have shrunk to a point where they disappear, along with time and space, and only my heart exists, thudding loudly and powerfully.

Nevertheless, after the hugs and laughter, after tears of happiness, my body does reappear and reminds me of the price I will pay next week for achieving these moments of joy now. However, tomorrow is not today.

the windy city | 4

I wake up all of a sudden. I don't know how many hours I have been asleep; I don't even remember stopping to stretch out to get some sleep. I only remember running over snow. It was a dark night, the kind where the cold creeps into your bones. I had kept on, one step after another, trying to find the trail in the blizzard.

However, I feel warm now. Outside, the storm seems to have died down, and high in the sky the sun is melting the snow and warming the rock walls of the shelter that has shielded me against the cold night. I am next to a meadow sheltered by 60- to 100-foot-high cliffs. To the right, a small fir wood protects the meadow from the fierce easterly winds. And beyond the meadow, a broad balcony extends before me, opening up a vision of valleys and green peaks that finally fade and give way to the plain.

This shelter is a stone building. It isn't big enough to call a cabin, but neither is it small enough to be a kennel. It comprises four walls made from large blocks of granite piled 5 feet high. There is no sign of the passage of time; the rock is new and still retains bits of mud and grass from when it was dragged out of the ground. Shepherds or hunters must have built this as a shelter for autumn nights like last night. Inside, a floor dug out of the ground with pick and spade protects against the cold of wet grass and allows you to stand up straight, as it adds an extra foot of space. A few handfuls of straw and branches on the ground along with a blanket that has likely endured countless freezing, rainy nights mean that I can stretch out fairly comfortably.

As I lie there and savor the early warmth, my mind drifts to another shelter from many years ago, though I remember it as if it were yesterday. During a long excursion into the Pyrenees, exhaustion and twilight reached us simultaneously. Alba complained she was tired and sleepy, and I let her talk me into finding a barn where we could shelter and spend the night before making a brisk descent on Monday, before sunrise, to get to work on time.

Alba and I met in Barcelona, which seems paradoxical given that we were two such spirits of nature. I had left my soothing mountains to go down to the city for a stress test. At the start of each season, all athletes had to go to a clinic in Barcelona for a medical checkup to monitor heart performance and to ensure there was no problem that might prevent us from continuing our physical activity. For years my heart performance had remained stable, but each year I went down for an electrocardiogram. To see how my heart responded to stress, I would do the Bruce Test. It's no Bruce Springsteen concert, but rather a run on a treadmill that increased speed every 3 minutes and was on an incline simulating an uphill slope. You had to run until your legs and heart couldn't stand the rhythm for another second, stopping just before the moving belt catapulted you to the other end of the room. All of this while wearing breathing tubes to connect your respiration to the doctors' computer and stickers on your chest to measure your heartbeat.

Although I hadn't noticed any changes that year, my doctors persuaded me it was particularly important to do the tests this time, after a very demanding summer, because they feared I had overtrained and overstretched myself. The doctor hadn't minced words: "If we see that you have overdone it, you'll have to give up training for at least a month until your levels return to normal."

All that had put me under enormous pressure and worried me terribly. Not training for a month would be like the end of life. What would I do? Unfortunately, a stress test isn't like a race, where you can smile and hide your true physical condition from your competitors. Computers don't lie.

In the end, despite all my worrying, the test results were perfect. There was nothing to indicate that I hadn't recovered from my fatigue following recent races.

I left the clinic, light with relief as I ventured out into the hot streets of Barcelona. As my car was with the mechanic, I'd traveled down by bus and would need to wait a long while before I could catch the return bus to Puigcerdà. I took a leisurely stroll down the Diagonal to the station. I got there an hour before my bus was scheduled to depart, so I sat on the station steps reading the latest book my sister had recommended and finally surrendered to me after I'd nagged her about it. The novel combined life stories of several protagonists who lived in different parts of Europe at the beginning of the twentieth century, before and during World War I. Time flew by, and I didn't notice that my bus had parked in its bay and was now loaded and preparing to leave. As the last passengers put their suitcases in the luggage hold, I jumped up and rushed onto the bus.

"Don't you worry, lad. I wouldn't have left you stranded," the driver said as I showed him my ticket.

The bus was full. As passengers arranged their backpacks on the racks, I went to the back and found an empty seat. Behind me, a group of young people about my age were shouting and shifting in their seats as they made plans for the great night out ahead of them. In front of me, an elderly couple was heading home from La Boqueria market with all the purchases they were going to cook for their children and grandchildren who were coming to dinner. The bus drove off as my thoughts wandered from these contrasting conversations to the book I was eager to get out of my backpack and resume reading.

All of a sudden, the driver braked sharply. We had gone only a few yards and hadn't gathered speed, but one of the boys behind me fell down in the aisle because he'd been standing. The doors opened and a fragile young woman got on looking very flustered. She was slim and not very tall, simply dressed in blue jeans and a green cotton T-shirt. She was carrying a gray backpack hanging by a single strap.

I confess that the first thing I looked at when she climbed on was her shoes. From what people say, I imagine that must be the consequence of professional tunnel vision. The shoes we wear say a lot about us: whether we like to walk, if we value comfort or style or something in the middle, if we like to feel tall, if we're all-purpose or city slickers. She wore white sneakers.

Her face was what most surprised me, hidden as it was behind long brown hair. It was delicate, very gentle and pale, and I expect that's why she seemed so fragile on first impression. Her eyes were dark blue and sparkled with life; she looked alert, but sad. As she made her way up the aisle, her slenderness and small stature emphasized her fragility, but her arms and the muscles that tensed under her jeans gave you an idea of her strength. She walked confidently but cautiously, as if she were out of place and not in her preferred environment.

She sat next to me—it was the only open seat—and as I bent down to take the book from my backpack, she exhaled and said to herself, "At last! I couldn't stand a moment more in this city. Who would ever want to live like that?"

"Well, I imagine 6 million people do. Though I can't really understand why either. Have you been in Barcelona for very long?" I responded.

She looked over in surprise, as if realizing she'd asked the question out loud instead of in her mind. Her eyes weren't as dark as they had seemed at first.

"Four hours, give or take a few minutes," came her reply. Her voice matched her build: gentle, and not at all shrill, more like a loud whisper.

"How many hours did *you* stand it?" she asked with a smile.

"Sorry, I have to say I beat you by a long stretch. It wasn't easy. There were difficult moments, lots of suffering. I was on the point of giving up several times . . . but in the end I held out for seven hours!"

She burst out laughing, and neither of us opened our books for the rest of the journey.

As we made our way up through Llobregat, the bus emptied out and dropped all its passengers in the satellite towns around Barcelona. Our conversation was relaxed and pleasant, and we didn't realize we were almost alone until the bus stopped and the driver stood up.

"Last stop! We're in Puigcerdà!"

The five remaining passengers got off the bus. I am shy and have never been good at saying good-bye. The easy flow of words

I had enjoyed over the three hours' journey seemed to depart along with the empty bus.

"Well, it was a pleasure meeting you. I don't know many people who think like you."

"The pleasure was mine. I don't know many people who hate the city either," she said with a laugh. "I'm just passing through Puigcerdà. But I'll be here for a while. I don't know how long, a few days or a few months. . . . I have to see whether I like it here." She stopped to take a breath. "If you come down to town, you're in trouble if you don't let me know!" She laughed again.

"Thanks. You'll soon find you like it here. It's a fantastic place. And if you come up to Font-Romeu, give me a ring. If you like skiing or hiking in the mountains, it is idyllic. . . ." It seemed as though our conversation wanted to mesh, wanted to find words and reasons to continue, but after a few minutes and a quick exchange of telephone numbers, we went our separate ways.

I picked up my car from the garage and drove up to Font-Romeu. I spent the entire drive thinking about the conversation and debating why I had said this and not that, why I hadn't had the courage to tell her that I liked her, that I thought she was fantastic.

I arrived home. Like every autumn, it was almost time to rotate wardrobes, to put running and cycling gear in suitcases and get out my ski kit. However, it wasn't yet cold enough to ski, and there were still hot days when I could go out for a bike ride and cold days when I had to wrap up well to go out for a run, so the house was piled high with kit. I lay on my bed and started to look at the results of the stress test, but my mind didn't want to digest information about oxygen consumption, aerobic and anaerobic thresholds; it could only think about a slim girl with a delicate complexion. I couldn't get her out of my head. And then it hit me: I didn't know her name! We had been so absorbed in our conversation that she hadn't told me her name. Now I had an excuse to call her; I grabbed the telephone.

"Hello?" I heard that same gentle voice and laughter I felt I'd not heard for days, though it had only been an hour ago.

"I'm sorry, you didn't tell me your name! Don't tell me now. What about telling me tonight over a drink or two?"

"Hey, great idea! Ten o'clock in the belfry square?"

I walked up and down the streets in the historic part of town, pretending to window-shop or watch Cerdanya by night from the Town Hall lookout point. I even read all the advertising magazines I could find, trying to make time fly by. However, time moved very slowly, almost as if it had stopped. Minutes passed like hours, and it became more and more difficult to ignore my thoughts, which were continually focusing on the moment when I'd meet her.

She was sitting on the terrace outside the bar, gazing at the illuminated belfry tower, her back to me. I watched her as I drew near. She was the only person on the street, and I could tell she was relaxed. Though it wasn't quite cold, the autumn nights were beginning to get cooler in the Pyrenees and people preferred to be inside benefiting from the bar's central heating.

I came up quietly behind her and leaned down to speak softly into her ear. "I'm Kilian," I said. She got up slowly, still gazing at the belfry. She turned around and stepped closer to me. In the soft light in the square her blue eyes looked bigger against her white skin. She looked me straight in the eye; her gaze was calm and serene.

"Alba," she said slowly and tenderly, inviting me to share in the stillness that her voice and gaze communicated. We stood and stared at each other, only a few inches apart. I don't know whether that lasted seconds or several minutes. Time seemed to slip by around us but had stopped as far as I was concerned, hooked by the power of her gaze. My pulse beat faster and louder. I could feel each heartbeat in every part of my body: my head, my hands, my legs. I felt as though my strength was draining from me and I was tottering. My legs were stiff but shaking, as if they couldn't bear my weight. If I had carried on like that for another second, I would have collapsed to the ground. For a thousandth of a second my pupils deserted her perfect eyes and centered on her pale pink lips. They looked so delicate as her cheeks broadened into a faint smile. I don't know if time was still at a stop or suddenly accelerating wildly. Our faces slowly drew together, leading the way for our bodies. My lips separated to let air reach my lungs so that I could gather strength. I noticed the heat our bodies were giving off. Sweat began to dot my forehead, and I felt as if I needed to take off my shirt despite the cold invading the streets as night fell. Our gazes crossed from lips to eyes, and my strength faded even more. It wasn't only my legs that were shaking now; my hands seemed heavy and awkward, and even my lips were trembling. I began to worry that if no one came to prop me up, I actually *would* fall to the ground. She was the one who brought me that support with her lips, and then I wrapped my arms around her and lost track of who was supporting whom.

I will never understand how people can live surrounded by cement, concrete, asphalt, iron, and glass. It is difficult to find a single reflection of what the earth used to be like when years ago it followed its cycles without interference, safe from mankind. What happened to the water that ran free and cut its own paths between the rocks to find the best way to reach its destination, the sea? Or to the flowers that struggled to survive among trees and bushes, vying with other flowers to steal that ray of sun that would allow them to show off their magnificence? Animals can no longer move freely across the terrain, are caged in by the man-made borders that now bisect their once wide-open lands. They can no longer simply follow the instincts to find shelter, seek out their prey, create their own hiding places in order to elude their predators—they can no longer live as they were meant to. And what about us? Aren't we basically just another animal? Like dogs, cats, and parrots, aren't we also trapped inside four cement walls that prevent us from flying freely, from being able to feel the human essence within us, the animal sleeping within that is waiting for the moment when it can wake up and run through a space of its own?

Our parents took my sister, Naila, and me on a hike across the Pyrenees on foot when I was 10. In those 42 days we discovered that we knew nothing at all about the mountains where we had lived all our lives, and that we loved them—though we didn't realize it at the time. When we made that trek as young kids, I didn't know that a seed of an idea had been planted in my unconscious that would finally begin to sprout in the spring of 2010. Timidly but firmly opening a path through the snow, that idea kept growing robustly until it started to assume a shape. Initially, it was like a fragile snow flower that was at once vulnerable and accessible, but as the months passed and it seemed as if it would begin to bear fruit, it began to look more like a mighty sequoia that was at once imposing and inaccessible—it was the idea that I could run across the Pyrenees in seven days. It had taken root so strongly I couldn't shake it off; night and day my thoughts were about my trans-Pyrenees run. There was no going back. The mountain ski season had finished a few months ago, and the peaks were still covered with a thick mantle of snow, but the desire driving me to the Basque Country to start this adventure was so powerful that rational reason hid behind blind desire and I couldn't restrain my body, which was heading west, following its instincts.

DAY 1

Rains weep at the break of dawn on a Monday at the end of May, and I stand there, more fearful than confident as the giant waves of the Atlantic crash against the Cabo Higuer cliffs, ready to run until I can dip my feet in the warm waters of the Mediterranean. Any disappointment or discouragement we might have felt at a dismal departure in a downpour is erased by the extra dose of motivation we get from imagining what we might see on a long day that will take us across the Basque mountains and what we might discover over the next seven days. This is how we will start, cheered on by the team and runners who, despite the rainstorm, have come to see the kickoff of this adventure: a run across the Pyrenees, along its valleys and across its peaks, following the frontier between France and Spain until, nearly 500 miles to our east, we are reunited with the salty water of the sea.

It seems as if the sea doesn't want to let go of us when we emerge from the rocks of Cabo Higuer. We meet strong winds and rain, and I can't decide whether the water wetting our faces is thrown up by the waves when they crash against the rocks or is pouring down gleefully from the sky. All the same, we are here to run; no one said this would be easy, and we knew we would encounter problems. Indeed, as our odyssey begins, the rain apparently wants to remind us that nature and the mountains will be the ones to decide if we will reach the Mediterranean.

The clock moves toward 8 a.m., and the heavy clouds spreading across the sky convince me it would be pointless to wait for them to disappear before we start our run. I feel sure it's better to start with these difficulties and to hope that, as the days go by, nature will take pity on us and send a little good weather.

"You all ready?" I shout, hoping to make myself heard over the wind and crashing waves. Two local runners I have only just met have offered to share the soaking and accompany us on the first 6 miles before they go to work. The weather may be opposed to the challenge we are about to take on, but the runners are ready to give their all to help me pull it off.

"Of course!" I barely hear their answer through the storm, and I reply with a determined *"Pues entonces, vamos!"*

We cover the first miles and are quickly sopping wet. The waves of the sea are replaced by the streams of water that cars splash over us as we negotiate the Irati motorway and penetrate the mountains. We chat, and the miles seem to fly by as the rain turns into a steady drizzle that slips easily off our wet bodies. Greg and Yon accompany me on the first stretch of trail. The soft terrain, fresh legs, and high spirits make it easy to set a good pace.

All of a sudden as we are descending the ridge separating Ibardin from the Lizuniaga Col, the trail drops us into a grass field with no way out. We look at each other. For the first time since we left the ocean, we take the map from our backpack. Until now, we had let ourselves be led by intuition and had followed the wind eastward, but when there are small valleys with a thousand paths, intuition sometimes takes you to a dead end.

As a result of Greg's good navigation skills from his years of adventure racing, and Yon's knowledge of the terrain, we work out that we are south of the main trail that was taking us to the Lizuniaga Col. We have two options: We can either retrace our steps for 3 or 4 miles to get back on the right track or try to cut through the middle of the woods to the north. We are afraid the extra miles will take their toll at the end of an anticipated day's haul of 80, so we decide on the second option, convinced that we will find the right track in a few minutes.

We don't take into account the fact that the vegetation on the Atlantic Pyrenees is totally different from what we find back home. We immediately realize the shorter option won't be the quickest as we start on a steep descent where the undergrowth is so dense we can't see where we are putting our feet. We are in a kind of bog between large boulders and grassy thickets. Our feet are soaked, but apart from the odd thorn from wild rose bushes, the ferns and grasses caressing our legs is a pleasant feeling. We keep close together as we descend so as not to get lost in this jungle. The vegetation gets denser and denser as we draw closer to the river, which, like a cup of coffee, gathers all the dregs at the bottom of the valley.

With more pain than glory, we reach the river and decide that the best route out will be to climb back up the other side and follow the course of the river in the hope that at some point, nature will have forgotten to fill a gully that will take us 1,800 feet higher, to the path we are so desperate to find. Time has come to a halt, and I don't think there can be more than 60 miles to go before we reach Orbaitzeta and, farther on, 50 to cross these mountains and be able to rest once more. We have only just set out, have gone about 12 miles, and are already lost and wasting minutes, precious hours of rest. If we continue at this rate . . .

But are we really lost? Don't we in fact want to lose ourselves and, like when we were kids, melt into the forest and discover its plants, animals, and life close up as a way to probe our inner selves? At this moment, though, my mind is far from esoteric reflections. I have only one thought in my head: crossing the distance between us and the path we have been chasing in circles by the river for at least half an hour.

After going upstream for a good while, we finally leave the river when we find the gully we have been searching for. Our legs and bodies recover their energy in our elation over finding a path to lead us out of the insecurity of the natural wilds and return us to civilization, even though the latter only expresses itself in the shape of a track that is barely a few feet wide. It all seems very contradictory. When we started on this trek, our aim was to go far into the mountains and find their wildest, purest, most natural depths, to distance ourselves from all civilization, from what mankind has built or destroyed, turning our backs on the world we have constructed during our existence as a species. Yet here we are, stripped of artifice, cut loose from humanity, finally experiencing what we so craved, and we feel unprotected, defenseless, and vulnerable. Fear creeps into our veins like a kind of adrenaline, anticipating the feeling of a leap into the void, the loss of control over our emotions and body. And as this situation drags on, fear of being lost, of not finding a way out, of being suddenly attacked by a wolf, becomes real and scary. Irrationally, we look around at the slightest sound or movement we hear. We look for an exit, scared of dying defenseless, surrounded by nature.

I think it is fear of death that frightens us when we lose contact with what is man-made. Our family and friends accustom us to the safety of the rational world, where every element focuses on the protection of our own, and when we are cut off from that shelter, we feel vulnerable, as if the path our life is pursuing could be interrupted at any moment by unknown perils. It is irrational, but the love we feel for humanity takes over, makes us feel we belong there, cradled in its arms. That feeling accompanies us everywhere, keeping us safe, yet at the same time muting the instinct that allows us to explore beyond its frontiers.

We shout at the tops of our voices as we emerge from the sea of vegetation and reach the safety of the main path. In a calmer frame of mind, we reestablish the pace that will lead us to the Lizuniaga Col, Lizarreta, and Erratzu. Gradually, in the rain, we draw near to the refuge where we will spend the night. Energized by the passing miles, time flies by as we catch up on what we have done in our lives and what we are planning for the future; before we realize it, we reach the ridges above Orbaitzeta as night falls.

We have reached the end of the first stage on this adventure, and our legs haven't suffered too much. After nearly 87 miles and more than 16 hours, the night is pitch-black and there's not much time for us to eat a plate of pasta or for David, the physiotherapist accompanying me on the whole of this trek, to massage my legs before I go to sleep sometime after midnight.

DAY 2

Night has dispatched the clouds and rain and made way for a bright day. What it couldn't dispatch was the ache in my legs, which, instead of improving with sleep, has gotten worse. I put on a brave face, determined to hide my pain from my colleagues, who are waiting for me to have breakfast before we start back on our run. What would they think if they knew my legs were hurting after the first day? It would demoralize the whole team! Their faces show how thrilled they are to start on this project with the expectation that they will carry it through. What would they feel if we had to go home after a single day? This isn't the time to show weakness, to suggest that the project hangs on a thread, that one stride too long, one slip and I am sure to tear a muscle. . . . No, now isn't the time.

So how should I react? Best to bury the pain. I don't want to dim the expectations I have placed on this adventure I feel so passionate about because of twinges in my legs. I'm sure it will get better over the next few hours or days. What with the rain and losing our way, we have piled up extra miles and *that* is what is taking its toll now. From now on, everything will return to normal.

As these ideas buzz around my head, I begin to run with Greg in the direction of Larrau. A track leads us gently up to the high ridges of Abodi, and the good weather and fresh air seem to bring the blood back to my legs, which start to regain their energy, allowing me to look up from the ground as we reach the ridges. The view is spectacular. The first rocky peaks of the Pyrenees tower in front of us, behind Belagua, and, farther on, the horizon extends like a rumpled blanket of myriad shades of yellow before disappearing into the sea. The view gives me the strength to reach Larrau, and I anticipate that the morning will be a smooth run through pristine passes.

After a short stop to consume gel and isotonic drinks, we start our run toward the peaks of Mesa De los Tres Reyes and Anie. Joan and Edu now accompany us; they didn't want to miss out on the spectacular landscapes in this corner of the Pyrenees. The miles pass by quickly, eased by our conversation and the gently undulating grassy terrain that allows us to run at a moderate pace, as if we were crossing clouds of soft cotton. The pain that my tendons and joints were feeling this morning is forgotten.

Our conversations gradually fall away, not for lack of topics or out of shyness, but because the terrain gets steeper and steeper and we need to reserve our energy for breathing and footing. We concentrate on the 10 or 12 miles still left to go. Edu and Joan went back a while ago, and Greg and I are now facing the peaks on the Barazea. We started out almost six hours ago and have eaten nothing solid since breakfast. Feeling hungry and tired, we stop for a few moments to sit down and take a rest under one of the peaks. The track continues to climb a short distance until it reaches the peaks and then starts an immediate descent into a long valley that should take us to Belagua, where tasty rolls await us.

You do not make good decisions on an empty stomach. We are growing increasingly hungry, and when we sit and look at our maps, we see that if we continue to press along at our present altitude below the peaks, we'll reach the end of the ridge path and then an easy descent will bring us to the bottom of the valley, within a few minutes' reach of the rolls that keep taking shape in our thoughts. It is a perfect plan; we can cut half an hour off our hunger if we go at a brisk pace. We are pleased with the clever way we have oriented ourselves.

I don't know whether the image of those rolls was so strong and powerful that it blocked our vision or erased the valleys from our map, but half an hour later we are at the end of the ridges and facing a rocky valley where there are clearly no paths. Our disappointment is plain in the glances we exchange. We are completely on the wrong track.

As hunger is more powerful than disappointment or niggling thoughts about why we were so stupid as to leave the right path, I immediately vanish into a sea of granite rocks, and Greg waits up on the ridge for a sign from me before hurtling down the scree. I start to advance to my right, looking for a route that will allow us to make a safe, rapid descent and that doesn't hide any surprises, such as a ravine or unstable rocks that might collapse on our backs. I see a route about 100 yards from the plateau where Greg is waiting for a signal from me. I shout loudly into the wind at him, telling him to come to where I am now, and without a second thought I head down the scree.

The fine stone makes for speedy progress and is easy going. I take big jumps and glissade down over the pebbles as if this was a dune in the desert or a safe, no-risk slope of fine snow, a soft surface cushioning us from the impact of our leaps or falls. We let ourselves be swept along by our emotion and the ease with which we make our top-speed descent. We forget our legs are not German engines able to turn at more than 7,000 rpm. Two minutes and we are on the valley floor. In the end, our error hasn't lost us as much time as we had imagined—only a few minutes. We grin and race over the mile and a half of huge rocks and streams between us and the right path, the one marked out in red and white that quickly leads us to our rolls.

Most of the team is waiting for us in Belagua; they have thoughtfully prepared two wonderful rolls filled with tomato, ham, and goat cheese. We devour them before making more, which we also devour. Cookies and energy bars are the desserts to round out our meal and prepare us for the fact that we are only at the halfway point on this stage. It will be at least six or seven hours before we sit in a chair again.

The rolls have an immediate impact. Our strength and energy return and urge us to put everything into our run so that we can have dinner before darkness falls. Thierry accompanies us on the first few minutes of the climb through a dense forest of oaks, across soil that reveals a thick layer of leaves that fell last autumn and have hibernated on the path under snow that is now melting under the spring sun.

We keep climbing through a changing landscape. We leave the oaks and enter a wood of red pine then black pine that gradually disappears as we reach alpine meadows where rivers meander whimsically around the landscape's undulating contours. As we move on, the grass begins to disappear under the blocks of granite that increasingly fill the floor of the open valley, and then in turn the stone vanishes under a thicker layer of snow beneath our feet.

Now everything is white, to our right and to our left, over our heads and under our feet. Nature is apparently trying to homogenize the landscape by sending a thick layer of mist that blots out all sight of the terrain. The only point of reference is the slope in front of us. We keep climbing until the snow-covered slope changes direction and we assume we have reached the plateau. Fatigue is setting in, but in the mist and with no signs to indicate our route, it is no time to stop. If we stop for a few minutes on this plateau, there is a 50 percent chance we will end up going back along the path down the slope we have just climbed.

We start to go straight down across a broad expanse of snow that takes us directly to the bottom of the valley. I look at the map. There is a large flange of terrain leading to a depression where the valley starts that we must follow if we are to join the path that will take us straight to the cabins in Ansabère. As we cannot possibly get lost and must go several hundred feet to the bottom of the cirque to find the right path, we slip down on our backsides and make a swift descent. We proceed at top speed and in no time reach the bottom of the cirque, where all the glaciers that descend from the peaks and ridges come together. We start to run alongside the river, and I soon realize that Greg is finding it difficult to continue. He draws near at a slow trot. His face says it all: His eyes are glued to the ground, and he grits his teeth hard at each step to deal with the pain.

"What's wrong? Have you twisted an ankle?" I ask.

"No, it's my right knee. I get a stabbing pain with every step I take. I think I must have dislocated it. Can you pull on it?" he asks.

His pain is real: A dislocated knee is incredibly painful and makes it nearly impossible to continue. He sits on the ground and clings to a rock as I pull his leg as hard as I can to see whether the knee will snap back into place.

After a few pulls, the snap doesn't happen. However, our worst possible option would be to stay put. The mist has lowered the temperature, and we are a long way from any refuge or road. We have a moderate climb followed by a long descent to where Olivier and Thierry, who can help Greg, will be waiting for us. We run on slowly and reach the cabins in Ansabère, where hikers have just arrived and are settling in for the night.

"Excuse me. Are we going in the right direction to get to the top of the Lac de la Chourique?" I ask while Greg stretches his leg against some rocks.

"Sure, follow the valley on the left to the lake and then it's straight on up to the plateau. Are you all right?" they ask, clearly taken aback by our exhausted appearance, Greg's peculiar exercises, and our apparent lack of orientation, which cannot seem like the best state in which to climb those mountain peaks. *It is just as well these are the last hurdles we have to deal with today*, I think to myself.

The climb goes better, Greg's pain diminishes a little bit, and we are able to set a fast pace, running the whole way up to the col and the peak, where a spectacular ridge brings us straight down over the lake in Ansabère. It is a steep descent, and here his pain gets sharper, though we are moving very slowly. A path along the right shore of the lake gently slopes down to the Las Foyas ravine, where we find Olivier and Thierry, who stay with Greg. We weren't aware that time had caught up with us, that we only had three hours of daylight left. We are still 18 miles from Somport and 30 from Sallent de Gállego, where we are supposed to sleep the night.

We agree with Thierry that it would be better to spend the night in Somport and resume our run tomorrow. That 30-mile stretch would be too much for us now.

I still have some of the energy that the rolls provided and start briskly on the climb to the peak of Rincón. The path disappears, and I start to climb slopes covered in grass and slate that take me straight to the top. The cold but pure air, the energy that comes from being alone on a ridge, and the strong smell of wet earth motivate me to start running, leaping, and singing as I zigzag on the path along the edge of the ridge. The mist teases me, playing fast and loose, and the wind appears and disappears as I imagine I am hang gliding over the ridge.

I think you can experience no greater sense of freedom than what you feel when you run on a ridge that seems to hang in the air. It's like running along the edge of the blade of a sword, taking care not to fall over one side as you accelerate with every step to leave the blade and the danger behind, though at the same time you don't want it to ever end. There is danger, but you can think only of flying, of giving your legs the freedom to go faster and faster, letting your body dance as it keeps its balance. It doesn't matter when or where—you could be descending the ridge on the Bosses of Mont Blanc, the ridges on the Olla de Núria or Carlit—that feeling of freedom never changes. However, like everything in life, nothing is eternal; the ridge finally gives way to a descent that takes me to the Lapassia refuge, where a short but demanding climb at this stage in the day, after some 55 miles, takes me to the Arlet Col.

My phone rings. "Where are you, Kilian? I'm climbing up from Somport looking for you with a headlamp. Don't leave the path and then take the trail, understand?" says Joan. He is clearly worried by the darkness that is beginning to descend over the valley floors.

← I climbed the Breithorn (13,661 feet) when I was 7 with my parents and my sister, Naila, who was 6.

↓ One of my first races was the Pyrenees Walk, a 7.5-mile cross-country ski that I competed in with my mother. I was 3.

Running with companions is extremely helpful during long cross-country runs like the Tahoe Rim Trail.

← I try to be efficient at rest stops. Here, on the Tahoe Rim Trail, Sònia treats my blisters while I eat a plate of pasta, wash my feet, and learn about the next section of the run.

← I've actually fallen asleep while running because I did not want to stop. Here, a short nap snatched on the Tahoe Rim Trail.

⬆ Things began to fall apart in the last 30 miles of my Pyrenees crossing. Lotta and Sònia treat my feet while I eat to gain strength for the last stretch. A long way still to go.

⬅ Improvisation has been key to many of my successes. During my traverse across the Pyrenees, we had to find alternative routes to bypass bad weather or snow.

⬅ After the most intense eight days of my life, all my emotions erupted when I took a swim in the Mediterranean with my mother.

→ The tenuous light from a headlamp is my only company on the long night hours of the Ultra-Trail du Mont-Blanc.

↓ When you hit the tape at the finish line, you relive all the suffering and emotions experienced in a race, a feeling that erupts into a moment of unparalleled bliss.

↑ Here with American ultrarunner Anton Krupicka.

→ On my ascent and descent of Kilimanjaro, I could feel the great mountain's spirit in the air, the dust, the light, and the rocks.

Skiing enables you to enjoy the most fantastic, dizzying views, as seen here, on the Pierra Menta with Swiss ski mountaineer Florent Troilet.

Running through mountains enables you to dance with their contours, read their terrain, and fuse with their many forms—in this case, the Mer de Glace glacier.

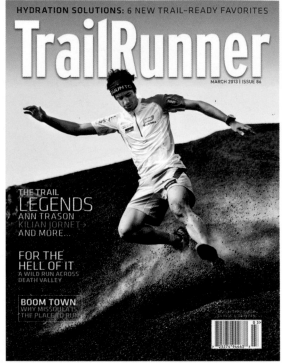

↑ Why do we run? This is a question often asked by people who don't run. For me, there is not one simple answer, but I think about it often.

→ I try to transform downhill stretches into a flowing dance between my body and the terrain, taking steps that flow naturally, as if they were an extension of that terrain.

↑ Once you have chosen your path, follow it confidently. Here, I run in one of the most spectacular places in the world, along the Tête aux Vents, during my first Ultra-Trail du Mont-Blanc.

I still feel strong and launch myself at speed along the small path to Espelunguere. I reach the cabin in five minutes and start running on the trail. The path is quick and direct; however, it goes into the woods, and the darkness under the trees won't let me run without risk of stumbling over a root, rock, or fallen tree. Although I can't see where it's going, the track is broad, so I take big, high strides to avoid stumbling.

I have been going downhill for a good half an hour when the telephone rings again.

"Hey! Where are you? Have you passed the cabin yet?"

"Wow, I must have passed it almost 40 minutes ago. Where are you?"

"I'm coming up the trail, on the right of the river. Can you hear the river?"

"Hmm . . ." I listen hard to my surroundings but can hear nothing. "I think it must be farther down, because I haven't passed anything, though the floor of the valley is beneath me, on my left . . ."

"All right, continue on down. I'm in a clearing that you'll see as soon as you leave the woods," Joan tells me.

Darkness has fallen, and I can now only imagine the silhouettes of the peaks. The forest is pitch-black, and running turns into an exercise in awareness. The trail zigzags violently down the slope, but the valley bottom always remains to my left. *I must cross it at some point!* I think. A quarter of an hour later, I'm on the bottom of the valley, by the river. I look in every direction, but see no sign of any clearing or anyone with a headlamp waiting for me. Only a wooden sign pointing to a path that goes up into the woods, where it says, "Somport, 50 mins. Cabañas de Arlet, 2h," and in the other direction, from where I have come, "Cabañas de Arlet, 2h 30 min."

I take out my phone.

"Joan! Can you see a signpost? How long does it say it is to Somport and the Cabañas de Arlet?"

"Wait a minute, I'll take a look." The line goes silent. "Yes! There is a sign. It says, 'Somport half an hour and Cabañas an hour and forty minutes.'"

"Is there another sign pointing downhill to the cabins?" I ask, wanting to confirm that I am where I think I am.

"Yes. Two hours forty minutes," he says, sounding surprised. "Where are you?" he asks.

"I'll be there in five minutes! See you soon!"

It is much easier making a descent with a headlamp; being able to see where you are putting your feet has a charm all its own. As I am running on legs that still seem fresh and am looking forward to a good night's sleep, the last miles on this stage to Somport zip by easily enough.

DAY 3

The alarm rings at 5:50 a.m.

What on earth am I doing here? Why didn't I go for a "normal" run rather than torturing my body like this?

As these thoughts go around my head, I try to get out of bed. *I'm still fine. I don't feel any pain*, I think, but the moment I start pressing on my knee to get out of bed, I feel a stab of pain under a ligament. *It's nothing to worry about.*

I get up, but when I stand up straight, my thigh muscles don't respond. I quickly sit back down on the side of the bed so that I don't fall. I look at the clock: 5:55 a.m. I have no time to lose. I get dressed slowly and carefully, trying not to move my legs. It's like dressing a dummy, a stone statue, even though I am the statue being dressed.

It's 6 a.m. I can't spend any more time feeling sorry for myself. I force myself to stand up. If I keep my legs straight and don't bend my knees, I can walk without my thigh muscles giving out. I feel as though I could fall to the ground at any moment, but I leave the bedroom. Joan, Thierry, and Sònia are waiting outside. I manage a smile to hide my distress. My mouth looks calm and confident, but when I look at my colleagues' faces, I know my dark, sunken eyes must show my pain and tiredness.

It's cold outside. When I open the door, the river of thick mist flowing between the valleys rushes into the shelter. I'm not sure if it's the rain that fell during the night or the early morning frost or the drizzly mist, but the fields have turned into marshland, and given the state of my feet, it isn't a good idea to spend 15 or 16 hours with them underwater.

The first steps I take are terrible. I shut my eyes at each step and monitor my breathing with every movement I make. I take small, slow steps and advance almost imperceptibly, like an injured bird that is unable to fly yet refuses to come to a halt and drags itself along, stubbornly trying to continue on its journey. I cover very little distance in a minute, and each step sends a violent pain through my body. When I put my foot on the ground, I feel the liquid in the blisters on my toes stinging and I grit my teeth. Small stabbing pains spread from my knees to my hamstrings and even as far as my hip.

I stop gritting my teeth and close my eyes, relaxing my face muscles in an attempt to fly to a world where pain doesn't exist. My thoughts carry me to distant beaches, hot, seaside days when all I have to do is sleep under a palm tree and listen to the waves that gently lap over my feet. The water is warm and cures my blisters. . . .

It's hopeless. The sound of the waves becomes rougher, colder, and gloomier. Everything goes dark, and when I open my eyes, the wind is still blowing mist between my legs. I am climbing. The path that was earth and grass is now mud and water and fading quickly into the mist, as if to emphasize the fact that our steps are ephemeral, that they will be imprinted on the mud for a few seconds and then erased by the mist forever. These thoughts nearly make me forget the cold, the blisters, and the pain in my legs.

When I reach the point where Edu is waiting for me, we don't need to say anything; the way I stare at the ground makes it obvious I am in another world, trying to make the miles speed by while my mind is elsewhere.

The descent brings me sharply back to reality. The first steps jolt me out of my dreams. Aches in my joints triggered by the climb turn into painful cramps in my legs and stomach. I don't have the reserves of strength to withstand the throbbing, and my mind molds my surroundings, sculpting the pain even onto the landscape. The earth has changed into hard, vertical rocks. The mist no longer seems a gentle haze but a sharp thorn slowly piercing my skin. It has gathered speed and strength and spits out rain that drives against my body.

Time and miles pass in between the mists and my thoughts. My legs warm up, and the pain eventually subsides. The dark landscape has lit up, and a warm sun is shining. The valleys have gone by to the accompaniment of conversations, beautiful scenery, and laughter.

As soon as the mist lifts, the sun blisters down and heats the valley floors to temperatures that were hard to imagine this morning.

I am now at the entrance to Ordesa y Monte Perdido National Park, sheltering by the fountain in the shade of a huge red pine tree and eating a big roll filled with goat cheese and mountain ham to give me strength for the rest of the day. It is 5 p.m. and time is starting to slip away. I say good-bye to my colleagues from the Bujaruelo refuge who accompanied me from there to the bottom of the valley. I look at my watch: We still have a long ascent and descent before we reach our next overnight stop. We have no time to waste, and I must make the most of the lightness in my legs and the absence of pain to make rapid progress.

I wet my T-shirt and hat in the freezing water spurting out of the fountain. I put my head under the gushing water and let it run through my hair, behind my ears, and onto my neck and back to cool down the temperature my body has reached in the last few hours under the sun and to freeze the gloomy thoughts that occupied my mind earlier but now seem so long ago.

Greg has volunteered to accompany me on the ascent to the Goriz refuge. It will be a long haul, so we start off at a leisurely canter. We are not far from the end of this stage, but something tells me that the day is going to be a long one and that I will need to draw on my energy reserves.

As we pass tourists coming down from the top of the park, we are cheerful and enjoying the run. But after we've been climbing for an hour, Greg starts to feel the knee problems from the day before. The stabbing pain increases, and he decides to go back. I feel fine and so continue at a good pace to the entrance to the Ordesa cirque, where I meet Jordi, a ranger from the Goriz refuge, who has come down to accompany me on the ascent.

A gulp of water, a few words of conversation, and on we go. My head starts spinning, set off by the heat and sun that have been like a furnace over the last eight hours, or perhaps it's exhaustion from the total number of hours I've been running. It is the third day in, and I can feel the impact from the miles accumulating in my body.

The spectacular vision of the Ordesa cirque makes me forget my fatigue. From north to south, a spectacular wall of rock looms before me that looks as if it must have been carved by Roman slaves in ancient times. To my right, the Punta de las Olas and the Pico de Añisclo rise up over the wall of rock. To my left, the spectacular Cola de Caballo waterfall unveils her imperious might and makes it clear that *she* sculpts these landscapes, that her waters can break the toughest rock and destroy whomever dares to mount a challenge, that she is the proud queen of her dominion.

Opposite me, crowning the whole spectacle, is the summit of Monte Perdido, sailing in the sky like Zeus on Mount Olympus. Sixteen hundred feet of sheer mountain wall rise vertically over green fields where cows and horses graze and wild animals come close to the edge of the river that flows calmly by. Marmots doze peacefully on warm rocks, bathing in the last hours of sunlight. The spectacular expanse of mountain wall contrasts with the calm at the bottom of the cirque. I am filled with a sense of peace and tranquility. My fatigue recedes into a distant past as the power of this place enters my every pore, filling me with its energy for my run across the green fields.

The climb to the Goriz refuge brings me back to reality yet again. The ascent is stony and very steep, and the distance seems endless. In front, Jordi keeps urging me on as the slope gradually flattens out, and we reach a balcony where the refuge is situated. The rest of the rangers and hikers at the refuge welcome me with applause and encouraging cheers.

"Where did you leave from this morning?" ask a couple of hikers who have just come down from Monte Perdido.

"This morning . . . " I think how distant that seems, as if several days rather than several hours had passed since we ran through the mist. "I started out from Somport."

They look at me, at each other, and then back at me. They don't seem convinced, but given the nods from the rangers and my very disheveled appearance, they seem prepared to accept what I said.

"Heavens! That's incredible. Congratulations. Are you going to stay here now?"

What I wouldn't give to stay here, to rest, to sleep, to eat. . . .

"No, I have to go down to Pineta."

When I was running uphill with Jordi, we had considered the various options that would take us to Pineta. Normally, by this time of year the Pyrenees have lost almost all of their snow, but after a very cold winter and especially a very cold spring with a lot of heavy snowstorms, the mountains are still completely white. And what had so far been slabs or cornices of snow that allowed you to glissade easily down now are becoming bigger hurdles that are difficult to cross, at least in running shoes.

We reduce our options to two by immediately discounting the possibility of crossing the magnificent Brecha de Rolando. Now, as we go up, we are left with the option of crossing the Añisclo passage or going up as far as the Cilindro passage. The first option is the most attractive to me: a long downhill climb but then only a 650-foot ascent followed by a 5,000-foot descent to the valley bottom. The real problem is that to reach the Añisclo passage, you must negotiate a long, very exposed ledge halfway up the wall from Monte Perdido and the Añisclo passage. The shelf is equipped with ropes and chains and is hewn out of the rock, an easy clamber in the summer if you are used to moving around in the mountains. However, it's currently covered in snow, and even if you were equipped with crampons, one slip (which wouldn't be difficult if you were in a rush) would send you hurtling down a 3,000-foot drop. That's why we decided with the rest of the team to choose the second option: a climb of 3,000 feet over uneven snow to the Cilindro passage, at an altitude of 10,500 feet, to cross over the Pineta Valley, where I'll have a 6,500-foot descent over snow and a couple of difficult passes.

This morning, one of the rangers, Piltri, had gone to explore the passage and had recommended I take an ice ax for the climb down. I follow his advice, and after eating a healthy omelet roll, I set out with Jordi in the direction of Monte Perdido. It's a steep climb, but the snow is hard and we make good, easy progress. I follow in the footsteps of my colleague, who runs up fast. I struggle to follow, reminded yet again that the rest at the refuge gave my legs only brief respite.

At the halfway mark, as the last rays of sun illuminate this paradise, Jordi turns back to the refuge. I take the opportunity to look up and enjoy one of the best moments of the crossing. At an altitude of nearly 10,000 feet, I am surrounded by giants made of rock that rest on the cushion of snow where I am perched. I am tiny, very tiny, a single black dot on this blanket of snow spreading under my feet. On the right, the Brecha de Rolando shuts the door on the final rays of light and leaves the Taillón in darkness. I follow the ridge and catch in front a glimpse of the Cola de Caballo waterfall, which now seems innocent and harmless among these giants. Beneath my feet, night begins to fall over the floor of the valley. The animals at the bottom of the cirque are no longer grazing or enjoying the sun, and the chamois have gone up the mountain to look for somewhere to sleep. One last look to record the spectacle: I would love to stay there, watching the sun hide behind the mountains that I have been crossing since morning, but night

is falling behind my back and the descent promises to be as entertaining as it will be dangerous.

An hour after leaving the refuge, I have just climbed the last 650
feet to the passage. I have kept up a good pace and earned myself
a few minutes of daylight for the descent, but a cool breeze warns
that the minutes of light will soon end, so I don't dally and begin
my descent of the icy slopes.

Because it is the east face of Monte Perdido, hours have passed
since the sun warmed the snow that has now changed into a layer
of hard ice. What might have been an easy descent a few hours
ago, glissading down on my backside, has turned into a perilous
down-climb on which I try to slot my shoes into the holes the hikers left this morning and dig in the ice pick to avoid a very proba-
ble slip.

Gradually, not making a single stop, I reach the real down-
climb. There is a pass between the rocks on a ledge some 50 feet
high where the ice comes to an end. The ledge is fitted with ropes
fixed to the rock with metal rings, and the crossing looks easy. I
grip the ice pick in my left hand while I position myself opposite
the mountain face and take the rope in my right. The strands in
the rope have worn over time, but it is still in a reasonable state.
In fact, it is probably not very old; it must have been put in place
the previous summer. However, it has been a harsh winter and
the rope has suffered from the many snowstorms and days of sun
and aridity that have gradually discolored its original green into
a rusty ocher. Even so, it looks strong, not one strand has broken,
and no knock from any ax or crampons has left it in a fragile state,
ready to break under a heavy load—although I imagine that after
losing the weight I've lost over the past few days, I could probably
hang from a woolen thread.

The snow that melted during the day has gradually penetrated the rope cover and soaked it. I put my hand on it; it's frozen! I nearly drop it, but then I tighten my grip and start my down-climb. The icy water trickling inside the rope leaks onto my fingers, but at least my hand doesn't burn when I run it along the rope.

I jump off the rock and fall on the snow. I leave the ice ax by the side of the rock for the mountain rangers to collect later and continue my descent. The slope is gentler now. It flattens out as I run down to the broad Pineta balcony. The light is almost nonexistent, but the sky is still clear, and the mountains are silhouetted perfectly around me. I leave behind Monte Perdido, and Cilindro de Marboré and the peaks of Astazou loom in front of me to my right. Beyond the extensive snowy balcony, night has fallen over the floor of the valley, where people are starting to switch on their house lights.

I can't afford to waste any time, so I run quickly across the balcony. The snow is hard, allowing me to move quickly forward, although now and then I tread or leap too heavily and the crust of snow breaks and I sink down up to my knees. It's been days since anyone took this route, and all footprints have faded from the snow. The path has been erased, but the truth is that the trail we are following to cross the Pyrenees doesn't exist, has yet to be created.

I decide to take the strip of rock on the right of the balcony. It's an easy descent: a snowy slope that gets steeper and steeper but that enables me to come down safely at a good pace. The tongue of snow is so broad it looks as if it must reach to the bottom of the valley; I clock up the feet at a fast rate as I slide and run down. The slope keeps getting steeper until, almost 1,000 feet beneath the balcony, the snow comes to an abrupt end and hangs over precipices that descend into the void, to what is now the black void of the valley.

"Shit. This wasn't the right way!"

I think for a moment. I can't get down this way. I must descend via the more easterly side of the balcony. The option of retracing my steps up the snow and across the balcony means I will waste a lot of time, and I have none to spare.

I finally decide to climb up the rock face veering to my right. It is an easy climb, though a fall would be fatal. I'm back on the balcony within half an hour and looking for the path again. It's not pitch-black, but I know it will soon be impossible to make out the terrain. I switch on my headlamp, but luckily it is a clear night and the reflection of the stars on the snow means that I easily find the marks from footprints that hikers left days ago in soft afternoon snow. Now, however, the expanses of snow that hours ago were welcoming, cottony blankets, playful and inviting, have turned into knives of ice, unforgiving and aggressive.

Worse, I can't chase Gerard Quintana from my head, who is singing lyrics that keep coming back at me: *"I'm falling. I'm gradually going. . . . "* I can't stop imagining and anticipating a slip, as if I were in a race, as if I were visualizing the course, my rivals, and even victory. Now I imagine the film scene of my fall in slow motion. I feel my foot slip on the ice, and my body starts to tumble down. What then? That's a moment that I can't envision, that I can't anticipate. I *can* imagine myself about to fall, trying to hold on to a hole or a stone to stop my fall and succeeding. I can even wonder what thoughts would go through my head if the soles of my running shoes lost contact with the ice. *Why on earth did you leave the ice pick at the end of that down-climb?* I am reminded that the decisions we make, however small and insignificant they may seem when we make them, *can* decide our fate. And once they are made, retracing our steps can sometimes be more tortuous and difficult than going on to find a solution.

Time seems to stop as I descend these hundreds of feet. Only five hours ago I was surrounded by people, cameras, food, and colleagues. The mountain seemed small when I had that entourage. Now I am alone. The mountain has become huge and imposing, and I am a mere leaf whose fate depends on the way the wind blows. But isn't that what we seek when we climb mountains, when we run along ridges and peaks? The feeling that we are human, puny and insignificant in this world when surrounded by the overwhelming might of nature. That we are like lost newborns searching for a mother's protection against a vast, strange world. In that moment we face the struggle to overcome or, perhaps, to go unperceived, careful not to wake the ogre slumbering among the giants around us, until we find our mother's arms.

lakes, rivers, and rain 5

The sun has reached its zenith and is slowly beginning its descent westward. The warm morning had seemed to augur a splendidly radiant day, but the blue sky has been clouding over and the mists in the valleys have settled over the peaks, leaving enough light to illuminate the landscape but not enough to make it a warm day. Hours ago, I left the idyllic cabin where I had spent the night. After so many sleepless nights, the rest has given me the necessary strength to continue my run and try to discover what I am chasing or what it is that is chasing me. All I know is that I must follow my instinct to find the right path.

The broad alpine meadows have disappeared from view and left me in much wilder mountain territory, where I now leap between peaks and canyons, from valley to valley, in the opposite direction of the path the sun is following through the sky.

People have always been confident that I would be able to achieve what I set out to do, certain that what was difficult for others is easy for me. That may be a result of the self-confidence I communicate, since I tend to see the positive side of things and react calmly to problems that crop up. I suppose I look as relaxed when I go down to shop at the supermarket as I do 10 minutes before

I set out for a world championship. And it isn't that I'm *not* sure of myself; on the contrary, I have always thought that I shouldn't feel nervous when I'm about to do something I do well and that, what's more, I practice and train for almost 360 days of the year. It's like a baker getting the jitters the day he has to bake bread. In the end, bread is bread and maybe the bread turns out good or bad depending on a number of things that escape the baker's control, but the bread will be made according to the same recipe whether it is Monday or Sunday.

Alba was the only person who didn't take this self-confidence for granted. She was able to see through this padding my subconscious gave me and find the insecurity gnawing beneath. Or maybe she just wanted to poke fun and hound me with the same questions that stirred in my own consciousness.

When I came home after training, the first thing I'd do was grab a jar of Nutella and devour it, spoonful after spoonful, even as I was imagining Alba behind me, waiting to scold me. And when I looked around, there she would be, arms folded, looking furious, though I knew she was only doing it to wind me up.

"Do you think you can win the world championships on Sunday if you put on a pound every day with your intake of chocolate?" she'd say in a deliberately angry voice.

"Hmm. I've just been training for five hours, and it was very cold today, so I burned it all up," I'd reply. "And you know that as far as I'm concerned, winning isn't what counts. There's more to it than that, and if I have to give up chocolate in order to win a race, then bring on defeat."

And we would burst out laughing and start in on a long argument about happiness, the importance of doing what you like, eating what you like, and living life with gusto. Although we share the same ideas, we still love to argue for hours on end between the kitchen and our bedroom.

In fact, it doesn't really matter what I do when I race. She has never come to see one, although she often went for runs herself. She knew that competition was a source of motivation for me, and despite not sharing that motivation, she understood it. I often encouraged her to come with me to run a race, but she would say she didn not need a number pinned to her chest to know that no one could beat her when it came to enjoying the everyday pleasures of being with nature.

Perhaps that was why I fell in love with her.

DAYS 4 & 5

The alarm rings again, for the fourth day in a row. The sense of physical well-being from the previous day and the dose of adrenaline during the final miles make me feel lively and optimistic. Days go by, and although it's still a long way off, the Mediterranean is drawing closer and closer.

After considering the problems we encountered on the first few days of the crossing—the harsh weather conditions and huge amount of snow on the highest reaches of the Pyrenees that forced us to change our route several times and to increase the mileage— we decide as a team to increase the length of the trek by one day. This gives me more time to sleep and recoup my energy.

Although this new plan relieves me of only 6 miles a day, the project seems to change radically. I leave in the mornings without the pressure of feeling I will be struggling at the end of each stage. In fact, the difference between a run of 68 miles in 15 or 16 hours and a run of 62 miles in an hour or two less may not seem like much, but it means that I have the leeway of an extra day, and that I can be sure I will see the sunset when I'm having dinner rather than from the last plateau on that day's run. Being able to sleep one or two hours more every night *does* radically change the character of my adventure. If my only worry so far had been wondering whether I'd be able to make it each night, I am now convinced that gradually, if I keep up a steady pace, we will arrive at the Mediterranean. My real worry, then, this morning is what shape my feet will be in at the end of the day, since I've been suffering from heel blisters. My knees are beginning to stiffen; my muscles are tired, and so is my heart.

After warming up on a 6-mile gentle downhill run to loosen my joints, we start on the long climb to make the leap to Benasc. I think how incredibly well my body is responding this morning after the way I suffered in the first hours of the run on my second and third days. Where is the pain hiding? Where are the shooting pains in my thigh muscles and the strain in the knees? What are they waiting for before they put in an appearance? Can my body have possibly gotten accustomed to all the effort? Or is it waiting for a moment of weakness to attack?

These thoughts vanish as I run uphill between Joan and Neto along comfortable paths among meadows and woods. On earlier days I've had to concentrate on simply taking one step at a time, eyes glued to the ground and gritting my teeth so that my muscles obey my thoughts, ignoring the pain. This morning, though, I can look up, surveying the landscape being warmed by the sun, following the animals running through the woods, or sprinting ahead to take a photo of my friends who are accompanying me. Or just enjoying the fact that I am running without having to think about my body or my brain—simply running. It has taken my body almost four days to start to enjoy this long trek to the Mediterranean.

Routine has set in, a cycle repeated from sunrise to sunset: My musical alarm goes off, and I wake up with my head buried in the pillow. A good breakfast of cereal and bread and jam to build up strength. I start running before the sun comes out, while it is still cool. I reach a steady pace, not so gentle that the miles stick to me like my sheets in the morning, but not too brisk so as to prevent me from enjoying the landscapes where we are leaving a trail of footprints. Benasc, Cerler, Bassiero, the beautiful lakes in the National Park of Aigüestortes, the lake of Sant Maurici, the Pallars valleys. I'm able to share all this time and scenery with friends who have come from near and far to accompany me and give me support.

I eat a roll at midday, then set off running again, leaving the cool of the morning behind. In the heat that hits this central part of the crossing, light pain returns—slight tendinitis in my feet and knees, small heel blisters or blisters between my toes that Sònia treats as they appear.

We go down to the valley bottom, where we rest before we need to switch on our headlamps, and we wrap up well against the low night temperatures. My legs are beginning to suffer the accumulated effect of the efforts I've been making day after day. A good plate of pasta for dinner while we talk to the rest of the team and to friends who have come on the run. David gives me a painful but necessary massage, and to end the day, it is back to bed and to sleep, thinking about what to expect in the morning and dreaming of moments we've experienced on the day that's just ended.

In this way time goes quickly, and without realizing, we have already reached the gateway to Andorra. As we start to climb the Tor Valley, I breathe in air I soon recognize. We've had a lot of routine days, getting on with it, making steady progress to the Mediterranean. In fact, I've had too many days like that and have forgotten the last time my legs felt pain caused by acceleration, the last time they suffered because they had accumulated so much lactic acid, which prevented me from taking long strides, lifting my knees high, and feeling my leg stretch behind in order to drive my body forward. I can no longer remember what my heart feels when it pounds so energetically and accelerates, bringing a taste of blood to my mouth, or how my breathing cuts out when it can't bring more oxygen to muscles that are clamoring for it. I can't even remember what speed is, and I miss it. I feel slow and heavy. Everyone is running shoulder to shoulder with me, accompanying my lethargic feet out of sympathy. Everyone can overtake me, accelerate, and help me while I stay steady and still, like a truck that keeps its brakes on downhill. I am easy prey for any predator—my senses are dozing, and my sharp reflexes and usual nimbleness lie forgotten in some corner of the Pyrenees.

My thoughts can't find a way out of this vicious circle; they make me feel even slower, crush me against the earth. My eyes fill with tears as I think how my stride is no longer that of a nimble runner who imagined he was a mountain goat leaping from crag to crag. I've changed into a bear that lumbers slowly and steadily. I have only steadiness, strength, and weight to protect me against predators. I don't like to feel like this: lethargic or that I must protect myself against myself. I begin to fight back. No. I am not a bear; I have always been a mountain goat. I *am* swift and nimble, and that is the spirit I carry within me. I want to feel that, need to feel that, or I will sink into a spiral of self-destruction: I need to know I can still fly.

I have been running with Marc along the riverside for hours. We have not said a word to each other in ages. It's not the place.

He is here to accompany me, to help me, and he gives me confidence and strength, the reassurance that I'm not alone, that I've got him if I need anything. He can urge me on if I'm tired or if my own mind is not up to it, can talk and argue if I need to be distracted from thinking about pain or monotony, can help to find the path, whatever I need. However, right now, I need to find *myself*, the rapid, self-starting runner I once was. That I *am*. I need to reengage with that unflappable spirit that enables me to ratchet up a gear when my body tells me I can't; that spirit that makes me continue the struggle when my thoughts are telling me to stop. If I am going to win a race, I need confidence in the knowledge that I can succeed. It's not rage, wildness, or the need to feel superior. It is the need to feel that I am wholly *myself* and not losing a grip on the person I was when I began on this crossing. I *will* take flight again.

The road to Tor starts to our right with a steep uphill bend. As I run uphill, my body, accustomed to protecting itself from physiological or muscular excess or the dangers of nature, slows the pace, reduces the length of each stride, and my breathing and my pulse flatten out. I accelerate, fighting against all this moderation. I'm fed up with so much restraint. My pulse accelerates, and my leg muscles begin to push so that I can lengthen my stride, raise my knees, and stretch my leg back to drive myself forward with every stride. My feet start to feel within each stride a movement powering me forward from my heel to the whip of the last metatarsal in my big toe. I open my mouth wide to take in air so that I can feel the air rushing against the walls of the trachea and the alveolus taking oxygen to my lungs. I breathe hard, blasting out air, then take in a fresh round. I straighten my body to let my lungs take in as much as they can, and my legs cover as much terrain as that new flexibility will allow, leaving my hip free to advance a few inches with every stride. I concentrate on my breathing, on keeping my legs moving at that explosive pace. My body is as straight as a rod, and my eyes seek out the quickest route, as if the road were a ski track and I a skier whose mind is set on how to attack the next stretch.

All of a sudden I realize I am running by myself. Marc has stayed back, and so has the film crew. I feel alive again, finally feel I am *myself*, and I am pleased; my spirit perks up at last.

The miles speed by, though the road climbs steeper and steeper. My legs accelerate at each stone wall I pass, playing with my lactic acid and giving me just the right amount to continue accelerating without having to stop, as if I've just come out of a sprint. I enjoy feeling the simultaneous sensation of being heavy and light, steady and explosive.

It's cruel to wake up from such a dream. My body has allowed my mind some 6 miles of frivolous entertainment, of blissful acceleration. However, when we reach the bucolic town of Tor, my body abandons me and leaves me no energy to feed my whims or strength to renew them. My body is neither heavy nor light: it is simply empty and hasn't the strength to go on. I try to eat and my stomach reacts violently. I do not have the strength to open my mouth or to utter even a single word.

But I'm back on home territory. Three miles on and 1,600 feet lower, I'll find Andorra, roads I know, and friends waiting to run the last lap with me. It's only another stage on this long cross-country run; I've still got three days to go, around 186 miles. But at the back of my mind, from the very beginning, I knew if I could reach this far, if I could overcome all the obstacles and find the way, I *would* reach the sea. Right now, I have 3 miles to go, and a 1,600-foot descent.

We start off slowly, bodies bent, breathing silently, smoothly, our feet close to the ground, trying to ensure that our muscles do the minimum in order to cover the miles that they must run. We continue silently without looking at each other, only watching the light on the land as the sun starts to dip behind us. We leave the forest trail and go up though the woods. It's a steep slope, so steep we have to use our hands, grabbing roots and branches to haul ourselves up. It's a terrain I would love in normal conditions. It reminds me of when I was small and we played at climbing up to the most impossible places. That makes me smile, and gradually my spirits and strength return.

While we playfully climb these rocky, tree-lined slopes, always looking out of the corner of our eyes at the majestic sunset that brings its golden light to our faces and the grass on the path, I hear voices above our heads. It's not two or three people talking. It's not the team waiting at the top of the climb. It is the gleeful buzz of a large crowd. It gets louder and louder, and when we leave the rocks and trees behind and emerge onto the road, I find 40 or more people, mostly faces I know—from school and racing, friends and relatives—waiting for me and reaffirming even more strongly the feeling that I have finally returned home.

The sun's last rays have faded when I am only about 2 miles from the valleys in the Botella Col, the gateway between Pallars and Andorra—2 miles, however, between my adventure's failure or triumph, darkness or light. But my body doesn't feel the miles at all now that it is running in the company of friends, of my mother and my sister.

DAY 6

What has really changed since yesterday? How has my body changed? Has it adapted to my efforts? My body is as tired now as it was yesterday morning and the day before yesterday. My feet feel equally weary, and so do my knees and hips. So what has changed this morning? Getting up for breakfast wasn't tough, punishing, or miserable. My mind wasn't blank, and my eyes weren't lost in an infinite void. My first steps of the day weren't painful and tottering. So what has changed this morning? Nothing in my body, everything in my mind.

I set a good pace at the outset and from the very first minute make fast progress with agile strides. The valleys and peaks pass by, don't even register as I run up and fly down steep slopes, sharing every moment with colleagues, friends, and family who have come to run with me. Everything is easy today. I know the path and don't have to stop to consult the map; my legs lead me straight to tracks and shortcuts I have used so often when training in winter, summer, spring, and autumn. My body works away, advancing of its own accord, freeing me to talk, look at the scenery, accelerate in order to take photos, or find the best stride to cross a river that surges down after so much snow has melted in recent days.

The day passes quickly amid smiles, and before I realize it, I'm home, by the Bulloses Lake, behind the Calma ski slopes where I have surely spent more hours skiing and running than I have spent at home. I start to climb steeper and steeper ski slopes but keep running, keep driving myself on as I do every day in training. My companions start to walk and drop behind, but I continue to run; I'm home now and can run up this slope. I reach the top of Los Moros, where the view opens out over the Cerdanya. To my right, the Puigpedrós, Cadí, and Tossa d'Alp mountains. In front, Puigmal, Eina . . . I know every corner of this landscape. No secret, no animal eludes me. I had imagined this moment, had longed for it, had dreamed about it. I want to cry. I want to sit on the ground and look ahead in silence and think about every moment that has gone by. It has been a magnificent day; I have not felt exhausted, and strength of mind has finally overcome my body. But I find I cannot cry. Why? Don't I have any emotion or feeling left within me? Has my sweat consumed all the water I had left and, with it, the ability to feel? Has this trip finally made me insensitive to pain, suffering, and fatigue, as well as to the emotions and feelings they bring? Has the monotony finally neutralized all sensitivity?

As these thoughts buzz around my mind, my companions reach the top of the slope, and we start to go down into the center of Font-Romeu, where everyone is waiting: friends from university, training, and school; teachers; shopkeepers; and restaurateurs. Everyone has come to congratulate me and give me support to the end. But suddenly I am absent, lost in the mists swirling around my mind, looking for my senses. I want the pain to return, want even the suffering to return, if that is the only way to reclaim my feelings.

DAY 7

As if in response to my prayers on the previous afternoon, the heavens have unleashed a heavy storm to return me to reality and to signal that the previous stage had been a mere oasis on our cross-mountain run, a dream too good to last.

It is raining very hard. The water rushes through the streets in rivers that flow into the fields at the end of the town. We start running with Martin, a leading light in French biathlon who has recently returned with an Olympic silver medal. Before we even leave Font-Romeu, our clothes are soaked, and the cold penetrates the marrow of our bones. We run in tandem, not saying a word, trying to think about what lies ahead as we leave the safety of the meadows and woods to confront the mountain. An hour later we reach Eina, where the trail starts its climbs to the ridges of Núria, and from then on, we will face 25 miles over peaks before we return to the safety of the valleys.

Just as we reach the start of the trail, we hear thunder and lightning over the peaks and ridges that are swathed in a thick blanket of mist. It would be too risky to continue on at this altitude, far too risky. The rain hasn't stopped. On the contrary, it is pouring down ever harder as if to warn us off the peaks. We confer with the whole team, joined now by friends from Font-Romeu, Martin, and teachers from the university, sheltering under the open trunk of the car, trying to think about how best to continue. Sopping-wet skin and clothes are not the best allies against the cold, which is beginning to freeze our bodies, and we decide to continue the debate in a warm room with cups of hot tea in our hands.

We spread out and consult all our maps and decide that the best solution is to continue our route by going along the GR-10, turning off halfway up through Carança, to El Canigó, and thus joining the route we'd initially planned for tomorrow in Ceret. This option will allow us to continue safely in the rain, but it will add a considerable number of miles to today's stage. The five or six hours along ridges will now become ten or eleven twisting though valleys. In any case, the miles won't go any more quickly chatting in a warm room.

It's midday by the time I start running again, in light rain but with a threatening sky and black clouds over the peaks of the mountains. The extra hours of rest have refreshed my legs, and trying to make up the hours we have lost, I set off with Greg at top speed along the paths that take us through the woods to Carança.

The thick mist filters into the leafy woods, and we begin to have doubts about our route. With so many changes in our itinerary, we've barely had time to study the maps and are none too confident of the way, though we cling strongly to our intuition. By the time our doubts start to make us anxious, a shirtless young man with a beard appears among the trees, as if he's sprung straight out of the ground.

"Andreu!" I shout.

Andreu accompanied me on the central Pyrenees stages and has been a refuge guard for a number of years in Carançà.

"Follow me," he says. "It's quicker if we head into the woods."

He immediately launches us off into a fast run up through the woods, along a stream that avoids many of the twists in the trail, and up to Rodó in next to no time. We start downhill, and after several hours, the rain starts to pour down once again. The hours go by, as do light rain, hard rain, eating while sheltering from the rain, thick mist that erases the path and soaks our bodies, mud, slipping and sliding, and gradually the miles, until I am alone again, running under the mountain walls of El Canigó.

I feel good. I don't know if it's still the revival I felt yesterday or if the daytime cold has invigorated my body. But today I have recovered my sensitivity. It's not simply freshness and speed I have recovered but emotions and feeling. The moment I reach the northeasterly ridges of El Carlit, I can't stop tears from welling up, and I sit on the ground and take in the view.

Behind me the sun is sending its last beams across the ridges of El Carlit. But that isn't what brings me back to life, what makes me cry. I can see the sea again, for the first time since I left the Atlantic Ocean a week ago. In the distance, the Mediterranean appears before me for the first time.

I sit and wait, without thought, not reflecting on success or what we have achieved. I simply gaze at the wonder before me. Several thousand feet beneath me, the infinite expanse of the sea. Like an old man who has just returned home after many years in exile, I cannot help but feel moved by the panorama extending before me.

The sun has stopped shining on the rocks behind me, and the landscape is starting to fade. But I myself have just reignited, have rediscovered feeling and the strength to continue, and I am full of hope once more. I know where I am heading.

DAY 8

Waking up in the Els Cortalets refuge, more than 6,500 feet above sea level and a little over 60 miles from the nearest beach, is enough to give me the energy to persevere to the end. I start running, content with the knowledge that this will be the last morning that I get up not knowing whether my legs will respond, not knowing whether the pain has gone or will return with the first strides I take. Knowing that although I am in real pain, I only have to continue until the sun sets one more time is a huge relief that allows me to enjoy the adventure and indulge small whims, that allows me to make small concessions to a body that won't have to pay for them the next morning.

It's hard warming up my muscles under the hot sun, which has swept away yesterday's rain, but gradually they spring into action, and when we reach Arlès after a long descent, I am physically and mentally equipped to face the last 60 miles. I make a small stop to eat a tasty cheese roll and start off again as the heat continues and my legs clock up the miles. The landscape has changed radically, becoming steadily more arid and dry. We have left behind the meadows and rocks of the high sierra to tackle the woods of Les Alberes.

It's midday when I reach El Pertús, and we now face only one final obstacle before we can splash our feet in the cool waters of the Mediterranean: Mount Neulós. But joy hasn't completely taken over. The heat of the last few hours has brought back much of the pain I'd been feeling over the last few days.

The team and numerous friends who have come to keep me company on the last few hours start running up Mount Neulós with enormous enthusiasm, but though I try to look as if I share their glee, I'm beginning to feel ever-more-searing pain. As I run up the mountain, pain in my right calf starts to worsen, beginning not only to cramp but also to slowly stiffen. We finish the climb and I think the pain will end, but it has only just begun.

Accompanied by Marc, I start running along the ridges of Les Alberes, a sharp edge between the plains of Rosselló and the Empordà that spread before us as far as the sea. I try to forget the pain by contemplating the magnificent panorama and sharing with my companion the high points experienced on the run and the many other adventures I have had, and it works for a time, making me forget my woes as we enjoy the conversation and laughs or the breeze blowing us along as we fly across these ridges. However, at other times the pain stings and sears and makes me realize that by adapting my stride to stop pain from the cramp in my calf, I have now strained my left hamstring. I keep on slowly, try to lengthen my stride into a run, but not too much, to avoid that violent stab of pain when I overstrain my leg, a pain that brings on nausea and makes me want to immediately sit on the ground and immobilize my leg. I thus avoid any careless movement that would bring back the stabbing pain.

We arrive for the final food break, where the whole team is waiting for me, just over 18 miles from the sea, 18 miles from the end of suffering and the end of our adventure. I feel neither happy nor triumphant. Rather, I feel worried. Once again we are relishing the approaching end, and yet this is the hardest time. These final few hours are the most difficult of the whole run. The pain from my hamstring is making me feel dizzy and sick, and it hurts whenever I try to stretch my leg and put my foot on the ground.

"What should we do?" I wonder out loud, even though my only option is to continue. We've not come this far not to finish, to give up today, 18 miles from our destination.

I don't allow my body enough time to get used to the well-being brought by rest. And, above all, I want to ensure that the rest of the team doesn't notice the pain I am in or how tired I am—even if my face makes that obvious. I start running very fast, with lots of rage. Probably too much rage. I can't feel the ground, the branches catching against my legs, or the rocks hitting my feet. I can't hear the voices of Marc, Pere, Pau, or Joan, who are talking behind me. I see only the images I want to see, those that enable me to continue to forget the pain and make me think that what I feel isn't important. I think of Dick Hoyt, a triathlete with a son who suffers from a bone-marrow disease that has left him paraplegic. So that his son can experience the joys of life just like anyone else, Hoyt runs Ironman® races dragging his son in a boat behind him on swims, transporting him by bike, and pushing his wheelchair on runs. I picture fierce battles in the Middle Ages, when soldiers ran and dragged themselves along when wounded; even though they'd been severely wounded, they never lost the energy or strength to continue. If they could do this, if people can stand so much pain, why can't I? And so I enter a spiral that has only one outcome as far as I am concerned: the sea. Nothing else exists. I am no longer myself; my reason is no longer in control of my steps and thoughts. Pain has induced a blindness to everything around me.

The miles pass very slowly, and my colleagues can see that I am dragging my hamstrung leg more and more and am slowing down. It's not yet pitch-black when we start to see the lights of Llançà. It is at this point, when Joan realizes I've abandoned all reason, that he decides to bring me back to the real world and rescue me from all those medieval battles and life-and-death struggles. He puts his hands on my shoulders, lowers his glasses, and looks me in the eye. I can hear his breathing, and his voice brings me back to consciousness and reason.

"You have achieved great things, Kilian. You don't have to prove anything to anybody."

I know I don't *have* to prove to anyone but myself that I can do it. I *want* to prove it.

"I know you can get there today; we know you can reach the sea in two, three, or four hours, and that it's not a problem for you. However, do you really want to get there today and provoke an injury that will stay with you for the whole summer, if not winter as well? Don't you want to keep running through summer? Don't you want to be able to do all those projects and races we were talking about only a few hours ago?"

He is right. It isn't about being heroic. It isn't a matter of proving to anyone that you can conceal pain; I'd already proved that to myself. We must be able to identify the difference between when our body is in pain because of the effort it has expended and when it is asking us to stop to avoid more serious consequences. The problem is that, in those moments, pain usually has the strongest voice, and to avoid it, our thoughts take us elsewhere, where colors don't exist, where there is only black or white. Life or death.

Eight days and three hours after leaving the waters of Cabo Higuer, my feet leave the sand on the beaches of Llançà to enter the salty water of the Mediterranean. Only an hour ago I was on the Sant Miquel, sitting with Thierry and Sònia listening to "Island in the Sun," our thoughts far away, looking out and remembering the moments we experienced this week. The host of memories sailing through my head made me feel as if we had set out months before. Rain in Eina, snow over Goriz, thickets in the Basque Country, morning in Somport, Tor, Andorra, friends, food, heat, cold, blisters, joy, and sorrow . . .

Today there are only tears. Tears of joy? Perhaps they are, now that I can see we succeeded at last and can relive all these moments that will remain in my memory forever. Remembering the people who helped me get this far, remembering conversations and images etched in my mind.

Tears of relief? Very likely, with the peace of mind brought by the knowledge that tomorrow I will get up and not have 62 miles on my agenda and that I won't suffer if my legs hurt when I get out of bed or worry whether I will be able to reach my destination before sunset.

Tears of sadness? Perhaps that, too. Sadness at leaving the Pyrenees and abandoning a routine so charged with emotion, at abandoning days that seemed to expand into weeks.

I really don't know where the tears come from, but I let the calm and pleasure of living this moment fill my spirit for a few minutes before setting off on the path that will finally take me to the sea.

My legs feel light without the burden of knowing that many miles still lie ahead. I don't have to manage reserves of strength, and the massage I had yesterday evening and the hours of rest seem to have erased all the pain I felt last night. Now I only have time for a pleasant run with friends and family, in this last hour before we leave these mountains.

a victory for the senses | 6

We were in bed after a fantastic day's training, and my eyes were still sparkling as I recounted the day to Alba. I was under the quilt and started talking, telling her what I had done and seen on the training session, reliving it, whispering when I wanted to suggest my fear or exclaiming jubilantly and even getting out of bed to show how exciting it was: "It was beautiful when we reached the top. The sun started to come out from behind the peaks, lighting up the glacier I'd just climbed. Then, because I was feeling good, I wondered, *Why don't I scramble up the narrow gullies to the right of the black needle?* I started climbing and it went well; I ran all the way. If I'd been competing in a race today, I would have performed extremely well. The views were incredible! I could see every single lake, could see our house down below, a speck. And all that snow on the descent! What a descent!"

She listened silently, taking in the story I was recounting so dramatically, and smiled at me from her place beneath the quilt. When I had finished my lengthy tale, I asked how *her* outing had gone.

"Fine," she said simply.

"What do you mean, 'fine'?" I asked, somewhat surprised. "You must have something to tell me after such a wonderful day! How did it go? What did you see?" I insisted, and she replied, in that self-assured way of hers, "You can tell your story and people will see it through your eyes. You can take photos and they can hear the birds singing and the snow moving the branches on the trees. You can write it down so they can feel the wind on their faces or smell the wet earth. But you can never get them to truly feel the excitement you felt when you were there. You can't make them cry as you cried or make their hearts beat as fast as yours did."

Then she smiled, turned away, and quickly fell asleep, leaving me crestfallen.

Alba was very strong. Maybe too strong. I craved finding something worthwhile in the things I did, and I couldn't do them and then feel gratified only within myself. I needed someone else to value what I had done. I needed to be told I had just been on an incredible hike. To be congratulated when I had won a race. I needed only a gesture, a look of approval, to give me some self-satisfaction and motivate me to train the next morning. I needed the people who loved me to feel proud and celebrate my good results, for my friends and acquaintances to acknowledge and remember what I had done so that I could feel sure of myself and more at peace. More simply, I needed to create a past so that I knew where I was coming from and could continue to move forward.

Alba needed none of this. She was able to feel self-confident and fulfilled simply by the emotion she experienced in the moment, a moment that she then forgot when her body could no longer feel it, and so she'd seek out another. I don't mean by this that she lived only for the moment or aimlessly. On the contrary, she was able to trace out a path in life without needing herself or others to create a past. On the one hand, I admired her and marveled at her inner strength; on the other, she made me feel inferior. I couldn't act like that, however much I might have wanted to. I felt the need to communicate what I had done, seen, or felt. Consequently, mostly to annoy her, I would say she was selfish, that she saw and felt incredible things and shouldn't keep them to herself, that she should share them with other people.

"Why?" she would reply. "What's the point of telling others about things that they couldn't have seen, that they will possibly never see, about feeling things that others haven't felt? Just so you can feel you are superior? To make it obvious you have something they don't? That you have experienced much more in life?"

I told her it was exactly the opposite: that it was so that people would keep on searching until they saw and felt it themselves. But our argument was never-ending.

I haven't seen her in a long time. The memory occasionally plays tricks on us. We eliminate what's painful and only remember the moments of euphoria. This happens with training sessions, too; from one year to the next, you only remember that day when you managed a series of impressive feats and felt good, or the week when you were able to sustain a very fast pace for six hours a day. You never recall the days when you struggled and were longing to get home, jump into bed, and forget your training. Rather, you always think that you were much better last year and that this season you've been laboring under pressure, exhausted by effort expended on previous days or by bad planning. You are always worrying why you aren't feeling as good as last year. That was what happened when Alba and I stopped seeing each other. But on her parting shot before she shut the door, my memory is clear: "Where are your posters of Daehlie and Brosse? Where have you put your myths? When did you change your idols?"

Now, in their place, photos of my victories and trophies of every size and shape fill my walls and closets. The moment you surpass the people you idolized and become your own idol, the magic of sport is lost. Idols are reference points that act to mark out a path, to help you know what you have to work at and fight for so that you can emulate what they have done. And when you have succeeded, when there is only one person you can surpass, and that person is yourself, it means you have understood nothing.

Alba's departure forced me to think a lot about what I meant to myself. If I was the person I wanted to imitate, I couldn't see ways to improve, had entered an impasse, and couldn't gaze humbly at those my idol was surpassing.

When you lose your way, when the train you're on stops because it has crossed all the boundaries it wanted to cross, you realize you have crossed none, that no goal is real, that no victory is valid anywhere else but within yourself.

Alba disappeared from my life, but her leaving taught me that victories are what you as an individual decide they are, and that however many victories you achieve, in the end they will be of worth only to you. Everyone can be king of his own castle, but outside he is vulnerable and can lose his way. This did not discourage me at all; in fact, it gave me the strength to seek out new idols—the ones within each person. It motivated me to find strength and inspiration from those around me, because the winner isn't the strongest, but rather the one who truly enjoys what he is doing.

I managed to reach that state of pleasant equilibrium I had so admired in Alba, not by drawing on moments spent alone, but rather by delving deeper into the lifestyles of others, which inspired me to discover new paths to explore.

Mountains give us the time and space to rediscover ourselves, but we also use them to share everything and create cast-iron links to other people. I've never been able to decide whether what I practice is a solitary or team sport. The food supplies, pacers, and group runs surely make it seem like a team sport. But independent of all that, the question I continually ask myself when I run is "Who am I running for?" On the Ultra-Trail du Mont-Blanc, when I am climbing the Grand Col Ferret and haven't seen anyone for seven hours and can't see any runners behind me, why do I keep on running? Whom do I keep running for? Am I running for myself? If that were the case, when I was tired, I would stop to rest, would sleep and admire the scenery, which is what I like doing and what my body wants me to do. But, in fact, am I running for others? I know I no longer run simply for myself: I run in order not to disappoint my partner and the friends who urged me on before I ever arrived in Chamonix. For family and the people who came out and helped during the race and who expect me to succeed. Or at least this is what I tell myself. I think I tell myself that I do it for them, at least in part, so that the whole weight of my decisions doesn't fall on me. However, when I don't stop and I keep on running, I do so mostly because I want to prove to myself that I can do it; it's not the others, but my own self who compels me to keep going.

At 6 p.m., the Place Balmat in Chamonix is packed. It is impossible to walk down the streets, and people stick their heads out of windows and jam into doorways and come out onto their balconies. I try to pass through the crowd unnoticed by the photographers and fans who have come to see the most prestigious, legendary ultra-trail race on the planet, the Ultra-Trail du Mont-Blanc. Some people ask me for an autograph or want their photograph taken with me; everyone congratulates me and wishes me well in the next 20 hours. *Why are they congratulating me if we've not even begun the run?* I wonder. As I said, there is no difference among us on the starting line. You can't tell one individual from another based on what they have achieved in the past, but only by what they can demonstrate now. And we haven't begun yet.

I slowly approach the starting area and leap over the barriers. I look around. I am surrounded by great runners, and the mere sound of their names fills me with awe because they have etched lines of gold in the history of this sport. I anticipate a long, hard battle against all these faces made famous by sports magazines and against other elite runners who compete far and wide to get into these same pages as well. I look behind me, where thousand of runners are also waiting for the starting gun, waving their arms in the air. Like me, they've come to fight extremely hard, but it's not a battle in which they try to eliminate their rivals, but rather a battle among colleagues, where the struggle is internal and the rivals are the reasons to keep going. I am in the first row and don't like that; I move back to the fifth. I prefer to leave discreetly, and I believe the race will put each runner in his place.

While runners engage in animated conversation, the start gets kicked off with music by Vangelis, which grows louder and louder until the shouting is silenced by "The Conquest of Paradise." The emotion is visible on the runners' faces: tears, smiles, and sober expressions. Each of us feels excitement at embarking on one of the most incredible adventures in a lifetime, but we also feel fear, not knowing whether we can make it through to the end. Will our bodies and minds resist?

People charge off at top speed, maybe to reduce the number of miles as quickly as possible or because they're just letting themselves be swept along by the cheering crowd that is boisterously urging them on. I advance through the group, and as we leave Chamonix I am leading the race. I like to run a race from this position: feeling in control, as though no movement can escape you and you know what state every runner is in.

A group of six—all among the favorites—is quickly out in front. We talk about our race preparations, congratulate each other on our respective successes, and map out challenges for the future. Even though we have infinite topics of conversation, our words dry up as the pace speeds up and the slope gets steeper.

We reach Saint Gervais, where thousands of spectators are waiting and cheering from behind the barriers. It is all very similar to last year; however, this year I notice that the other runners look at me and talk to me differently. Is it because they see me as a rival now that I have shown my worth rather than simply because I am keeping pace with them? What a person is capable of doing in a race isn't expressed by past race results, but rather by what he does in this moment and the pace he sets now. Last year I was an unknown quantity, and many people thought that I was a mere sparring partner giving his all but that my bubble would eventually burst; this year they see me as an experienced runner. In the meantime, it is the same Ultra-Trail. What is the difference? What has changed?

Several hours later, I am alone. The lights behind me have disappeared, and there is only the night, the wind, and the path in front of me. I hear my breathing and try to keep it in time with my strides in order to establish a regular rhythm and a reference point to follow. I keep thinking about what lies ahead: In five minutes I will reach the col, in one hour the lake. . . . I try to find short-term goals to spur on my feet and keep moving forward. However, the hours pass, and in the pitch-black, time vanishes into the white circle of light from my headlamp. I enter a spiral that is difficult to escape, in which all external references disappear and the only thing keeping me in touch with reality is the beam of light illuminating the next yard of track. I become self-engrossed, and I begin to spin stories in my mind to give meaning to what I am doing. I am a fugitive fleeing the police across the mountains, a medieval knight escaping from the army pursuing him; I am chasing bandits who have set fire to my home. When day breaks, I am so deep into the spiral that I can't snap out of it and my mind comes back to reality only in occasional, brief moments of lucidity.

It is afternoon when, on my descent back to Chamonix, something pulls me up, brings me back to the world outside the walls of my mind. It is a moment I'd been longing for, because the run down signals the end, a return to reality. I feel the warmth of the sun on my skin and the sweat streaming down my face, hear my noisy breathing. I hear my name broadcast over the loudspeakers as thousands of people start to chant it. I feel the excitement rising. I want to cry and laugh, to shout out in joy, but I'm still not entirely in control of my body; part of me is still seeking a way out of the spiral. I feel dizzy. The light is so bright I can't see faces; there is so much noise I can hear nothing; there are so many hands touching me that I lose control of my own movements. It's all been too sudden. In only a few minutes I have tried to move from the utter solitude of my inner being into a world that is exploding outside of me.

I have always thought of myself more as a mountaineer than a runner, and you should climb to the top of a mountain only if you are able to descend afterward. To come down from the top after a race, you must forget yourself and everything around you so that you can organize your emotions after a victory, get back to work, and let go of the past. You can't prepare another ascent until you're all the way back down.

On my run today there aren't thousands of people chanting my name or cameras recording every step I take or my every word. Today I don't have to make any exceptional effort; nobody knows where I am, and nobody will know how it has gone. I'm skiing up to a needle of a mountain peak whose name I don't even know. I left home three hours ago with my skis, and after leaping a couple of cols, I found I was confronting a magnificent peak. I don't know its name or altitude, whether it is easy or difficult, who was the first to climb it or whether anyone ever has. Nevertheless, I can't take my eyes off this magnificent peak or stop my feet from taking me to its base as I search for the easiest way to the top.

I can see a rocky gully that goes nearly to the top, and it looks feasible. I'm sure it's not the most sensible thing to climb that gully alone, without informing anyone of where I've gone and not knowing how difficult it is or what dangers might lurk there, but I can't resist the impulse that's driving me to climb it. Why? Nobody is pushing me, and it's certainly not the best thing for my training. The only reason I can give is that there is no real reason. I can only follow the powerful urge driving me on toward it, as if it were a pretty girl with bewitching charms. I do it for my own sake because I must, to see if I can.

It's an easy gully, and I start to go up quickly as my boots sink into the snow and leave a perfect trail. As I climb up, however, the fissure gets narrower and the snow more packed. It gets harder and harder for my boots to get a grip on the snow, and I regret leaving my crampons at home. Nevertheless, I can't go back; the lure is too strong.

The snow comes to an end, and I start climbing on rock. My hold is fragile, and I have to ensure that my hands and feet are firmly in place and that the rock won't crumble. I take more than an hour to cover 65 steep feet. So why don't I go down? Why don't

I return home to safety? No one will know whether I've taken 20 or 21 minutes to get as far as the col, whether I reached the top or stayed on the col. Today I will get home, cook supper, and go to bed. And tomorrow I will probably forget what I did today, and no one, maybe not even I, will know if I ever got to the end of that gully.

But I can't turn back. It's selfish, I know. To endanger my life is selfish, not for my sake, but for all those who love me, my family, my friends, and all the people who have bet on me and worked with me. It is a whim of mine that could destroy everything. Why aren't they here with me now? Why isn't their force urging me to retreat? Could the force here be stronger, compelling me, like a lone wolf, to go after this goal and think of nothing else?

Perhaps it is best to strike a balance between these two forces in order to be able to continue running both for yourself and for others—but where is that boundary? What is the right balance between the desire to drive yourself farther and feel you are who you are, and pleasing others but in doing so, lose a part of yourself?

running a long way to find yourself | 7

I can feel the sinews in my right leg contract with every step, from the tips of my toes through my calves and tibia and upward to my thigh muscles as my heel makes contact with the ground. But the contractions don't end there; every fiber in my body is tightening, even as my brain sends out the order for them to relax, to stop acting in a way that strains my muscles, makes them throb. I feel stinging pain searing from my feet to my head. My leg is stiff, as though blood and muscle are turning to cement even as I desperately try to fight against it and break through the rock. I sometimes succeed, shortening my stride to prevent the cramps from spreading all through my body, reaching up to my arms, my back, even my jaw. I will my muscles to obey, but they ignore me, and my rigid, unmovable leg hits the ground hard, weighing a ton, not letting me soften the impact or even control where I place my foot. I fall but luckily am able to tuck in my legs and wait a few seconds for the cramp to subside before getting back up to try for another step.

My head is spinning, the light is blinding, and the intense heat turns to ice under my skin. I'm not well. I feel queasy, and that prevents me from making the simplest of movements without expending a huge mental effort. All of my strength, all of my energy, is focused on lifting my legs off the ground. I hear Jorge running behind me, urging me on. I know I cannot take my eyes off the spot where I want my feet to land, not even to glance at the sun hiding behind the California mountains.

It is as if I have to learn anew how to walk, how to move my fingers to grasp a cup of water, or how to control my muscles in order to keep from collapsing to the ground. I can't allow myself to relax, or even to think; I know that if I let my head get lost in thought, my legs will cease working and my body will crash down, limp and lifeless. I am like a wooden puppet that needs someone to direct it, to decide which string to pull to raise a leg so that I can move forward. The only way I can progress and prevent my legs from losing control and suddenly crumbling beneath me is to repeat to myself, *Small steps, no abrupt movements, gradually activate the muscles*, over and over again.

Thud, thud, thud. What the hell is that? All I've heard for several hours are Jorge's shouts urging me on and the voices of the volunteers when we reach an aid station. Now we are a long way from any station. There are 4 miles to go, and the last station was 2 miles ago. What is that noise? *Thud, thud, thud.* It gets louder and quicker. I can hear shouting behind me. Encouraging cheers? Jorge looks at me anxiously. "Come on, Kilian, give it your all now, we're almost there. Come on, go for it!"

Now I understand: They are footsteps. A runner is coming up from behind. I gather from the sound and the cheering of his pacer, which is getting louder and clearer, that he's closing in at top speed, like a cheetah running those last few yards before pouncing on a gazelle: he sees it, smells its scent, can almost touch it, and can't resist attacking it with a smile, with relish. Jorge looks at me anxiously. I try to quicken my pace. I can do it, for myself, for Jorge, who has come to keep me company, for the whole team. I really can!

But my legs won't respond. With each step I feel the sinews contracting again, as if they were glass needles, paralyzing my body. It is over. My strength has gone. My legs aren't obeying the orders I send them, and, above all, I've lost any hope I had. The steps behind me pound louder and louder, *thud, thud*, with rhythm and power. I clearly hear his foot smashing against the ground, accelerating with each stride, closing in on his prey.

San Francisco is an incredible, bustling, restless city. I arrived several hours before the rest of the team, so I have a whole day to enjoy getting to know the city. I don't waste any time at the hotel. I put my suitcase on the bed and leave it full, unpacking only my shoes, and head out for a run in a westerly direction in pursuit of the Pacific Ocean. I round the first corner and find myself on Market Street, in the heart of the city. It is early afternoon, and all kinds of people throng there: noisy students slowly heading home, tourists photographing a tram climbing the city's famous steep slopes, a group of shoppers exiting the Apple store, where they have bought the latest gadgets. I walk past a disheveled older man asking a group of young punks for spare change. It is hot; you can feel the humidity from the sea. But it's a pleasure to be able to run wearing only shorts and a singlet after weeks of training in long sleeves, hat, and gloves, where every breath made a cloud of steam. *Only yesterday, in the Cerdanya, you were returning from the Carlit with frozen feet, sopping wet from the snow on the high ridges!* I think, smiling.

I run along on Market Street until I reach Golden Gate Park, where all of a sudden the surroundings change from a bustling city full of tall buildings to a placid nature scene. I am surrounded by tall trees, meadows, lakes, lots of squirrels, and even the occasional bison (behind a fence, of course). There's no better way to get to know a city than to discover it through running!

I feel a light breeze as I draw nearer to the Pacific, and once there, I follow the coast northeast until I come to Golden Gate Bridge. Four hours later, after exploring the city and satisfying my desire for a run after so many hours on the plane, I return to the hotel to prepare with the rest of the team to head inland, to the mountains and the race.

The Western States Endurance Run is the most well-known, prestigious endurance run this side of the Atlantic. It is also a race full of interesting history. It was born out of an old horse race, the Tevis Cup, that was held every year from the most westerly point of Lake Tahoe in Squaw Valley to Auburn. In 1974 rider Gordon Ainsleigh, who was 27 at the time, noticed his horse had injured a leg before the race. Ainsleigh did not want his trip to Squaw Valley to be in vain and decided to participate in the race anyway—without his horse. The organizers were surprised, but convinced it would be impossible for him to finish, they let him run. Not only did he finish, but he finished in under 24 hours, not very long after those on horseback. From then on, the Western States 100 has been held as a running race over that same terrain, covering 100 miles.

The alarm goes off at 4 a.m. It's no struggle to get out of bed; I have slept well, and pre-race nerves make my body spring into action at the first *dring-dring*.

Out the window the sky is still black, though I can see a few points of light: the headlamps of the early risers who are out warming up on the frost that covers the Squaw Valley ski runs after a cold night more than 6,500 feet above sea level. The temperature in my bedroom is pleasant enough, and I need only a short-sleeve T-shirt. The clothes I will wear for the race are folded on the chair. I do a quick review to check that everything is there, just as I did last night before going to sleep: socks, shoes, shorts, chip, T-shirt with race bib already attached by four pins. Perfect. I take a quick shower to ensure all my muscles are alert, then eat a piece of energy cake for breakfast. It's half an hour before the start when I finally go down to the warm-up area.

I can feel the excitement mount as some 400 runners begin to pack into a few dozen yards, waiting for the race director to fire into the sky. I hear the cheering of a small band of spectators who have gotten up at 5 a.m. to watch the line of runners climb toward the snowy peaks. Some runners reply with enthusiastic shouts.

The run will last perhaps 16 hours for the fastest, but more than 30 hours for the less experienced. You can feel the tension in the air. But the tension is different than it is before the start of an important race in Europe, when the participants—from those who are chasing a prize-winning time to those who simply want to finish—are often quite agitated at the starting line, concerned about whether their preparation was enough or correct, whether the sacrifices made to take part in the race were worthwhile, and whether they will be able to finish in the time they have set for themselves. Every race is a matter of life or death, and you could cut the tension with a knife before the starting gun is fired. Here, in the moments before the start, it seems to me that none of the runners are thinking too hard about their body or how important the race is. Everyone seems caught up in the excitement of simply *participating* in this adventure. Though many runners are perhaps hoping to come in within 24 hours, what's more crucial here seems to be to enjoy the landscapes and to run at a comfortable speed; this is the method that will take you the farthest in this race. Gradually, the body, with the help of nature, will find its natural rhythm, and that will decide if you are capable of reaching Auburn and in what kind of time.

When the first glimmers of light begin to show in the east, from behind Lake Tahoe, and the sky begins to abandon black and assume various shades of yellow and red, a loud *bang* rings out from the barrel of a revolver, and cheers ring out as 400 runners set out toward the far west.

The first hours of the race are quiet. A dozen of us bunch out in front, talking about different races we have run, what impressions they left, whether we liked or disliked them, about our training over the last weeks, the equipment we are carrying, runners and friends we share in common. It is as if it were a long training run with a group of friends who have not seen each other for days and want to catch up on all the news.

In these first hours of the race, I think a good deal about whether I should go on the attack, taking up my fastest pace right from the beginning. I'm surprised by the laid-back atmosphere and pace of the race, which, despite being fast, is comfortable. I think how such a start would be impossible in Europe, where, even in a nearly 24-hour race like the Ultra-Trail du Mont-Blanc, we give 100 percent right from the start, with people spurting ahead in the first miles and every runner trying to waste the fewest number of seconds; after all, we never know if we'll need them later.

Here, in the Western States race, it seems as though a more reasonable, less aggressive and competitive order rules. It is as if a group of friends is out for a run, and at times a natural sifting out takes place as some slow or stop because they can't cope with the distance or keep up with the leaders.

And so in this way, without any spurts or marked changes of pace, the runners gradually spread out around mile 18, on the climb leading to Robinson Flat, until I am alone beside Anton Krupicka. Anton is a force of nature, a tall, slim runner with a long beard and chestnut brown hair, his body tanned by hours spent running in the mountains of Boulder, Colorado. He runs only in shorts and shoes, without socks or T-shirt, although, like many other American runners, he carries a flask of cold water in each hand. Geoff Roes, a runner from Alaska, runs just ahead of us, and though he is more reserved than Anton, I am impressed by his easy, simple stride, which looks so efficient.

As if we were tracing the hands of a clock, our strides follow a steady rhythm, *tick-tock*. Never making extra effort to climb a slight incline and never stopping to drink water, rest our legs, or eat. I am surprised by Anton's and Geoff's ability to sustain that constant rhythm, and also at how they never stop at food points or waste seconds eating cookies or slices of fruit or relaxing and drinking a glass of ice-cold water. They only stop to change their empty flasks for full ones and then continue on at the same rhythm, as simple as that.

The hours go by and our conversation trails off. I'm not sure whether it's because we've run out of topics, because we've said all we had to say, or because we are beginning to feel the time and miles on the trail; whatever the reason, we have all become more withdrawn now. The temperature rises as we approach the canyons, gradually but steadily, and I begin to feel the sweat streaming down my forehead, leaving a sticky layer on my arms and legs. My clothes begin to hang heavy, and at each food stop I need to douse my head in cold water and drink a lot of ice water.

Monotony is taking over. I'm not used to running on this terrain, with such broad, flat tracks. The early morning mountain landscape is now behind us, and for some time we've seen only fields and woods with lots of parched grass and dusty trails. The rhythm goes with the terrain; as there are no big changes in levels, every step is identical. Not a single longer or shorter stride, and never a slope to rush down or climb to attack. If you add to that the heat, which is increasingly unbearable, this monotony is putting me to sleep, leaving my body and, above all, my mind inside a bubble that's difficult to burst. I am a runner who likes to sprint, to change rhythm, to accelerate up steep slopes and rest or recuperate going downhill. This steady, monotonous rhythm is killing me.

Luckily, we soon reach the canyons, the only stretch of the race with significant level changes. We have to cross two rivers that cut across our route from north to south. The track narrows with slopes to go up and down every several hundred yards before it will return to another 70 miles of monotony.

Once we have reached the top of the first canyon, we start down a steep slope. The track zigzags sharply. Anton has been setting the pace in front for some time, and we follow on. Geoff is close on his heels, and I, in turn, am close on Geoff's, but surprisingly, the change of terrain doesn't seem to change the steady rhythm of my colleagues.

I turn up the volume on my iPod and look for a song. I tell myself that when I find it, I will start to go at my own rhythm. The first bars of Bach's Orchestral Suite No. 3 sound out, and I let myself be swept along by the melody and glide along the path, enjoying its twists and turns, braking abruptly a couple of yards before I reach each one and regain my rhythm halfway around the bend. I take advantage of obstacles offered by the terrain to be playful, to leap over them, to accelerate, to dodge them with my body . . . anything to break this monotony and feel that rush of adrenaline I seek when I run across mountains.

I look behind me after a few minutes and see no one. They've made no attempt to follow me on this downward surge to break the steady pace. I keep running down, enjoying the terrain and the opportunities it offers me to enjoy myself, as if, rather than running, I am on a mountain bike or my skis.

I reach the bottom of the canyon, and before crossing the bridge to start the climb, I go down to the river and cool myself down. The sultry atmosphere at the bottom of the canyon is oppressive, stifling my breathing. I dip my head into the river and also wet my hat and T-shirt, and with that short but efficient refreshment, I start the climb up with Anton just behind me. He has also accelerated downhill, leaving Geoff behind.

The heat shows no sign of waning as we run up—quite the opposite, in fact. At the top of the second canyon, the feeling of heat is so intense that I have to sit down for a moment and throw a bucket of icy water over myself before passing through weight control. At four or five spots in the race, when we reach an aid station, volunteers wait for us with scales to check our weight. If we have lost 10 percent of the weight we had when we set out, they will not allow us to leave until we eat and drink what is necessary. On this occasion, the weighing volunteers warn me that I'm at the edge of my threshold.

After the heat of the canyons, I feel a breeze beginning to blow along the ridge, which perks me up. I feel good, my legs are still fresh, and I have reserves of energy. The pace is fast but comfortable, and we're more than halfway there.

In Foresthill, at mile 60, the race ceases to be an individual adventure with other runners. From here until we reach the end, we will be accompanied by our pacers, or "hares," who will run with us. Though they can't give us food or drink, they will be a vital help in sustaining the pace and motivating us at the more testing times that come in the last miles of long-distance races. My first pacer is Rickey Gates, an American runner from Aspen who specializes in short distances and uphill runs. I have already worked with Rickey several times, in races such as Sierre-Zinal, and he has always brought good results.

As if it were a question of split seconds, with no time to eat or drink, Anton and I leave Foresthill with our respective pacers and enter the downhill part of the race. The early afternoon heat begins to feel intolerable, making it hard to breathe normally. Every time I breathe, the air burns my throat, and when I try to drink, the water I filled my flask with only five minutes ago is already boiling, no longer of use even to throw over my hat to wet my head. I try putting ice cubes between my hat and head, around my neck, to soak all my clothes in water, but the heat intensifies and my body cannot cool down.

My strength is still intact; the constant pace has barely punished my body, and I still have one or two cards to play that I intend to keep for later on. But dehydration and a lack of salt begin to take their toll as we start the run downhill toward the famous Rucky Chucky river crossing. I feel small twinges of cramping in my right calf, then in my left, and then other cramps begin in my thigh muscles. I've not stopped at a single aid station to drink and have eaten nothing during the race, not even a single roll or pie that might have given me the salts I need. Anton's and Geoff's rhythm, sustained by not stopping at the stations, led me to forget about eating, and I'm beginning to pay the price.

I try to chase negative ideas from my head. There are only 18 miles to go, and I need to make the most of my remaining cards at the appropriate moment. There is one final uphill stretch 6 miles from the finish line, which might be a good moment to use them, keeping just a scrap back for the climb in the last 3 miles.

I enjoy thinking through the tactics for my races, planning as I run. As I'm thinking about the strategy for these last few hours, we reach the river, which is in full flow with a heavy volume of water from the melting snows of California's Sierra Nevada. Given the flow, the organization has provided a boat to take us from the east bank to the west bank. The four of us—Anton, myself, and our pacers—clamber into the boat and make the most of these restful moments, relaxing, closing our eyes, and breathing.

On the other side, I jump out of the boat into the river. The water is cold and flows powerfully against my body, refreshing me, cleansing the sweat from my skin. My pulse also reacts to the cool and drops dozens of beats. I immerse my head in the river, letting the water run through my hair, soaking it. A minute later, I emerge refreshed from the river; the cool water seems to have revived not only my muscles and skin, but also my spirit.

I leave the water and begin running. Anton is a few yards ahead of me. I start running in order to draw abreast with him, but my legs don't react. It seems the water has not only cooled my muscles but has frozen the sinews, which are now stiff. I feel a sharp jerk that goes from my calves to above my buttock muscles, paralyzing my legs. My thigh muscles contract, out of control, straining all their fibers, a feeling that is accompanied by a sharp jabbing through my thighs, as if they were turning to rock. The pain is intense, intolerable, and makes me wish the muscle would explode and put an end to my suffering. *What is happening?* I think. *Has the cold water paralyzed my body?*

I struggle to reach the next aid station. There I find Jorge Pacheco waiting for me, a great Mexican long-distance runner who, after making the podium in this same race and winning Badwater several times, has come to accompany me on the last 18 miles to the stadium in Auburn.

I try to eat salts, drink water, and refresh my legs by doing a few stretches to keep them from cramping again, but I cannot prevent how the muscles are tightening to the maximum at even the slightest movement, and worse, it seems I cannot control the way my legs move.

We have just 18 miles to go. These 18 miles, which should have gone by quickly and been the time I went on the attack, have become more than four hours of despair and suffering. Four hours of summoning up energy, telling myself I can do it, breaking into a run, then 10 paces of falling to the ground, legs set in cement, eyes streaming from the pain. The pain is the physical pain of cramping, but it is also the pain of not being able to control my body, of not finding the solution that can give me hope. Feet, hands, arms, and even my jaw have joined in the symphony that, beyond my control, plays a baroque melody that is savage and rages free, not letting me pick up the baton of my body and direct it to its destiny.

So with minutes running in a vile temper followed by minutes walking in despair and minutes suffering on the ground trying to stretch my legs, the distance seems like miles and the miles like fragments of eternity. Anton and Geoff disappear over the horizon while Jorge and I continue to fight against this eternity in order to reach our destination. I know that when we pass through the gates to the stadium, that there, at the end of the race, will be happiness: happiness because I have fought to the end, happiness because I have taken my body as far as it could go. But for the moment, my whole body is completely paralyzed, like in a dream I used to have before my races, where I was slowly extinguished, becoming heavier and heavier until I sank into the landscape.

I can hear Jorge breathing just behind me as the sun sets in front of me. Hope is the last thing you lose, but my muscles have long since abandoned me, and my legs won't respond when I try to pick up speed. They forgot how to run hours ago and now can manage only a gentle trot that allows me to protect them against the spasms and cramps I've had over the last hours. For the first time, I turn around to check that the steps and voices I hear are not the fruit of my imagination, although Jorge's expression and nervousness had already confirmed for me that they are real. A large, sturdily built man wearing a yellow T-shirt, a white hat, and dark shorts and carrying a flask in each hand is running up a few yards behind me at a strong pace. Right on his heels, another man with long hair and a beard, also carrying two flasks, is easily running up the last slope in the race. It is Nick Clark; I recognize him from the presentation of elite runners the day before the race. We talked for a while then, but right now I can't even remember which state he's from.

I start to run on the right side of the path, leaving space for this perfectly synchronized couple to pass me comfortably without crashing into me. After a few seconds I feel the breeze blow on my back, and when I look up, I can see Nick's back moving along the path into the distance.

"Come on, Kilian. You've got to catch them now. You are strong enough to go faster; you can keep it up. You've done the uphill stretch, now only 100 yards, then half a mile, and then 3 miles on asphalt to the finish line. Come on, Kilian. He's tired as well."

I look into Jorge's eyes. I don't know if they are full of conviction or despair. Can I do it? I have to try. Even if only to go along with the wishes of my pacer.

My body stopped obeying orders hours ago. I breathe deeply and count to 10, close my eyes, and take in all the air I can. I stop staring at the ground and look up in order to focus on my objective. There is a cloud of dust some 20 yards in front of me thrown up by the perfect pair and, just above that, Nick's back. I won't stop; I will ignore the pain and won't look down until my feet are also part of that dust cloud. I accelerate, and my legs take a few seconds to react before warning me with short, stabbing pains and cramping that paralysis is imminent. But this time, my orders are stronger; I can break through the rock that wants to invade my muscles and brain. I focus on the movement of the back I'm closing in on. This is no time to worry about pain.

In the distance, as if separated by a wall of water, I hear the increasingly louder, more energetic shouts of encouragement from Jorge, who can see that his orders are working and that we are catching up with the American runner.

Step by step, second by second, the gap between us closes—only 10 yards now. *Come on! I can do it!* I repeat to myself. Now I can hear him breathing hard. He is feeling the effort he made when he overtook me. . . . 5, 4, 3, 2 . . . *I've got him!* I can't help smiling. *I've done it!* I glance at Jorge, who keeps cheering me on and congratulating me. I can see the pride in his eyes. I was able to defeat the cement spreading through my legs, and I am back in the fight. I've abandoned fear of failure and found the path of hope.

I take a more relaxed couple of strides to steady my pace and, feeling happy, resume normal breathing after making that supreme effort. I look back at the ground to concentrate on my steps and shut myself back into my bubble. At that point, I don't know if it is Nick who changes speed or if it is my legs that take back the control from my mind, but suddenly, as if punishing me for the impudence, my legs start to powerfully cramp, reminding me that they will be the ones who will finally decide what place I take in this race. I don't know quite what happened, but I know that Nick's back has now run on far into the distance where the sun has just set.

I didn't come here to give up hope, to stop fighting when, only 3 miles from the finish line, my body says, "Enough." I didn't come here for my body to dominate my mind. Where is everything I learned from running the Tahoe Rim Trail? What about what they say about the brain being the most powerful muscle in the body? Where is the power of the mind that can eliminate pain and achieve incredible things? Can't I run 3 miles at speed under pressure? Didn't I do a vertical race only four months ago, sick with a fever, and didn't I last out and fight to the final minute, on the attack, sprinting? Didn't I struggle every morning when I was crossing the Pyrenees? Yes, I can run for 15 minutes and bear the pain, the suffering. I can give it my all to reach the finish line exhausted but happy that I have given the best of myself. I can do it!

I look up from the ground. My objective is no longer the back that continues at that same rhythm a hundred or so yards in front of me; my objective is now the Auburn stadium. I breathe hard, take in all the air I can, and breathe out forcefully. The race starts here, now, with only 3 miles to go. My legs begin to respond. With each stride I struggle to overcome the stiffness and to avoid a fall. I feel as if I am breaking the chains imprisoning my muscles, and with each stride, I drive them harder, gaining speed. The chains finally break, falling from my body and allowing me to move more freely, to flow.

Within a few minutes, I have almost drawn level with Nick, but now is not the time to stay close on his heels. I am now nearly shoulder to shoulder with him as he and his pacer just stare at me in astonishment. A hundred yards on, I begin to hear the shouts of encouragement from the last aid station in the race before we join the roadway. From then on, only 2 miles of asphalt on the flat, with a slight uphill incline at the end and a half-mile slope down into the stadium.

Nick matches the pace I have imposed and runs next to me, elbow to elbow, not letting me pass him. As if it were merely a mirage, we pass the aid station without stopping and turn as quickly as we can onto the asphalt. The 100-mile race has become a 3,000-meter chase. There's no time to think about hydrating, or to watch how night falls on Auburn, or to debate with our pacers, who are shouting like madmen behind us. We keep elbow to elbow, staring straight ahead, not wanting to look at each other and betray any sign of weakness.

It isn't about overcoming a rival in these last yards, after so many hours of solitude, but rather about proving to myself that I am capable of giving my best, of telling my body that it can still run fast, that I can reach the finish line content, knowing I couldn't have put even one more ounce of energy into it.

On my right, Nick begins to accelerate at top speed—more than 11 miles an hour. He moves ahead, but not so far this time that I can see his back. Fifty yards and the slight asphalt incline begins. I decide that here is where I will mount my counterattack on his sprint. I start to take deep breaths, to stretch my legs long, trying to gather strength. Now is the time. I increase my pace. I begin to feel the uphill climb and draw on every bit of strength I have left. My breathing increases, my chest is about to explode, and my legs are running wild, making it difficult for me to control the cramp that's invading my calves. But I think only of accelerating; there's no point in turning my head to see where Nick is. Looking back loses you vital tenths of seconds and breaks your concentration. Jorge starts shouting like a madman that I'm leaving Nick behind me. I grit my teeth and accelerate faster. Ten yards, the final yards before the downhill stretch into the stadium, then only half a mile left before turning right and starting on the athletics track.

It feels like the longest half mile in my life. My legs begin to rebel, Nick is right behind me, and the stadium is nowhere to be seen. Another stride, going faster and faster. I can't look back; I can't look at the ground; I must look ahead, only ahead. Finally, the entrance to the stadium looms before me. I close my eyes for a moment and take a deep breath; now I can say that I have succeeded, that I have given everything, that I have fulfilled my desire. A turn to the right and I enter beneath the bright glow of the floodlights that illuminate the final yards of an adventure that began early this morning 100 miles to the east.

In my final strides, I thank Jorge for giving me strength when my mind had none and greet the spectators who have come to see us make the finish. I cross the finish line and fall to the ground; my legs cannot tolerate any more of the fire burning in them, and they abandon me to gravity.

A good friend of mine once said that you learn little from victories; on the contrary, when things are going badly, when the situation is hard and it's difficult to get out, when you've made 99 attempts to get up and have fallen back 99 times, and at the 100th have managed to find a solution, that's when you mature and really learn something about yourself. Injuring my kneecap had been a terrible but significant moment in my life up to then, a turning point. The Western States 100, too, taught me a lot about myself. On the very practical side, it taught me how to feed and hydrate myself more efficiently. But much more importantly, it helped deepen my understanding of how my body and mind work and how to better fight back.

we celebrate a peak when we're back down

8

Although it has been less than three months since my American adventure, it seems very distant now when viewed from 13,000 feet above sea level at the Barranco Camp, beneath the summit of Mount Kilimanjaro. But the desire I feel is the same as I felt in the United States: I want to challenge myself, give the best of myself, and try to discover what my thresholds are, to know myself better. In Tanzania, the thresholds I will test don't relate to heat and distance; here it is about how my body will react to altitude and speed in a more technical terrain.

I've never liked to restrict myself to a single pursuit; I think that limits the ways you can get to know yourself. I don't mean to imply that I like to do a little bit of everything but do nothing well; quite the opposite, I like to prepare the best way I can for whatever I do and to be as competitive as possible. But variety of activity allows us to explore every corner of our body and mind. I like the taste of blood in my mouth when I'm competing in a relay race or skiing in a vertical race, just as I like to feel the loneliness of the long-distance runner. Each activity reveals something new about myself, and not simply about my body. It's obvious, if you've been running for 40 hours and then collapse, that 40 hours is your threshold. But what use is such knowledge to me? No use at all. However, the things that my body has learned during those hours and, more importantly, how my mind has been able to motivate me to concentrate during that time, even in moments I thought it was impossible, will forever be of use to me.

Knowing I can run 3,000 feet straight uphill in 30 minutes isn't of much practical use in a world in which technology can transport us at unimaginable speeds, but it does help me to know that my muscles are able to function when they lack oxygen, to know that I have an ability to concentrate 100 percent, to know that I can successfully fight to achieve what I set out to do. The goal may be a vertical mile, or an ultra-trail, or a marathon, but it can also be about playing a piece of music, finishing a painting, solving a theory, or carrying out research. The result isn't what's important, but rather the path you must take to get there.

The path is very obvious here in Tanzania, where the air surrounding us feels completely different from the air in the rest of the world. It seems we have returned to our origins, where nature imposes its laws and humans are the ones who must adapt to go forward. Here, I will ascend and descend the magnificent Kilimanjaro in what I hope is a record time. We will see what nature allows.

We have been sleeping in tents for a week to get used to being at this elevation and are now fully into the routines of tent life. Day-to-day life is straightforward and is about doing only what is necessary. We get up in the morning when the warm sun starts penetrating the canvas of our tents, and after a short medical check to measure the oxygen in our blood, our breathing, and our pulse rates to confirm that we are adapting well and to discount any likelihood of altitude sickness, we go eat breakfast in the meal tent. Tea and hot ginger help keep us warm in the cold that comes down from the glaciers and are fine accompaniments to the toast or pancakes with honey and jam that give us energy to begin the day.

We fill our backpacks and help the porters fill the sacks with the gear necessary for camping, and we gradually start to move on to the next camp. It is remarkable to see the porters walk so skillfully up between blocks of volcanic rock and huge tree roots, balancing sacks of more than 40 pounds on their heads. They move forward slowly but surely, stopping for short breaks to give their necks and shoulders a rest from the weight they are carrying.

Once we reach the camp, we erect the tents and kitchen in a few minutes before preparing lunch, and we wash in a bucket of cold water under a warm sun. In the afternoon, everyone is free to do what they want and what their bodies require: some rest in their tent; others walk around the camp and take advantage of the magnificent light and views to take photographs or simply sit on a rock and watch the colors in the sky change as the sun sets. Simon, the expedition guide and record holder for the ascent and descent of Kilimanjaro, and I use the time to run to higher altitudes to acclimate my body to making that effort with much less oxygen.

I have adapted well from the start. I have had no headaches and have been able to run easily uphill between 13,000 and 19,000 feet. My body seems to be reacting well to the lack of oxygen, though the truth is that with views like these, it is difficult to listen to your body when your mind is so filled with contemplating the wonders. Earlier, on an afternoon training run from Barranco Camp, I was surprised and utterly charmed by the sight of the sun projecting the shadow of Kilimanjaro onto the savannah extending before me, 13,000 feet below. The shadow drew a perfect triangle, darkening the cape of bright gold that swathes the whole mountain. In that moment, I really began to feel that I am on the ceiling of Africa.

To the right of the shadow from Kilimanjaro, a single obstacle halted the spread of the savannah: Mount Meru imposed itself as if it were fighting against Mount Kilimanjaro for domination over the plains of Africa. I looked at the ground, trying to leave the dreamlike vistas awakening in the distance, but the incredible gilded light that illuminated Barranco and the looming protrusion of volcanic rock known as Lava Tower wouldn't allow me to turn my gaze away.

Perhaps the most surprising feature of this trek, though, isn't the play of light on incredible landscapes or the whimsical shapes of the lava, but rather the constant cheer displayed by the porters. As the days have passed, the trust and convivial feelings between the Franco-German and Catalan team and the Tanzanian porters and guides has grown. On the first days our exchanges were few and brief—"Jambo, how are you?" "Good, thanks"—but as time has passed, the conversations in broken English and the universal language of signs have taken on more depth. We are no longer the porters on one side and the Europeans on the other: We have melded into a single team.

From the start, we have been surprised that the porters always have a smile for us. When loading up the heavy sacks between the rocks, when cooking dinner in the dusty camp, when getting up at 6 in the morning in 5°F temperatures after spending the night in a tent without a sleeping bag . . . they are always smiling and happy. The landscape deserves such an attitude, though I imagine that after you have looked at it day after day, it ceases to be exceptional and simply becomes the backdrop to everyday life. The work is very hard, but they seem to take pleasure in it and in the fact that they can participate in the dreams of climbers who perhaps help them realize some of their own.

The conditions are difficult: wearing battered rope sandals and clothes salvaged from what other climbers have given them at the end of a descent from the top, sleeping in a tent in all the clothes they own because they didn't have warm sleeping bags, and always being away from their family, week after week, expedition after expedition. But after talking to them, I realized that despite all of this, they *do* appreciate the beauty of these landscapes, and they enjoy seeing them through the eyes and words of foreign visitors experiencing them for the first time. They enjoy telling visitors about how, years ago, the glaciers reached 3,000 feet farther down, as far as Barranco, and that before the cities became so enormous, you could still see lions running wild across the savannah.

I learned that they dream of being able to travel, of finding better work so that they can install electricity in their homes or buy shoes for their children. Iddikenja, a porter who was just 30 but looked a good 10 years older, wanted to earn enough money in two years to be able to go to the capital and study to be a guide and then lead groups up the mountains. Or China, who was a great fan of snowboarding, although he had only seen snow on the glaciers of Kilimanjaro, he followed the sport enthusiastically by looking at photographs in magazines. His eyes were full of dreams when he saw pictures of the snow-capped Pyrenees and Alps and videos of mountain ski races.

We have just come down from the peak for the first time and are tired but content as we arrive back in Barranco. Today we went up with the whole team to scout the last section of the route, and everyone had specific tasks: the camera team—Olivier, Raphael, and Marlène—to find the best spots for filming; Stephan, to take the best images; Sònia, to acclimatize herself, as she would be the one who would have to help me in case of an accident or if I got altitude sickness; Thierry, to find places from which he could see the route and give live coverage; and my father, who, after taking clients on a climb to the top the previous week, had joined the group in order to participate in and add his experience to the adventure. Three porters and Simon completed the team that would lead the way and carry medical supplies, scout the final stretch to the top and the descent, and complete a last training session before the real attempt. However, as we approached the top, we began to lose any sense of what we were supposed to be doing and became absorbed by the astonishing scenery and by the fact that we were flying high above the continent of Africa. Whichever way we looked, at eye level there was only sky. It is a difficult feeling to describe—a bit like the experience of victory, when you know you have succeeded, you are ecstatic, can feel your hair standing on end and your pulse racing. We could all feel that tingling sensation as we touched the top of Uhuru, more than 19,000 feet above sea level.

After an energetic flurry of welcome from the porters who had stayed back at our camp, and after checking that we have all returned in a good state, I begin to get the equipment ready that I will need the day after tomorrow when I start my attempt on the record from the Umbwe Gate. There is very little to get ready, and in an hour I have my backpack filled with all the equipment I must take down with me, a canteen of water, and a couple of energy gels for Greg and Stephan to give me when I pass by Barranco. I will also give them a jacket and gloves in case the temperature drops on the final stage, since it was only about 5°F at the top this morning.

For Sònia and Thierry, who will wait for me at the top, I leave only another canteen and some cookies, since the descent from there will soon return me to warmer temperatures where I'll not need my outer layers.

The last backpack includes the kit I will wear and carry from the start: shorts, a short-sleeve T-shirt, an energy gel, sunglasses, socks, shoes, and my iPod. I also pack what I'll need to spend the night at the entrance to the national park: a sleeping bag, a toiletry bag, a thick jacket, and long pants. I shut myself in my tent nice and early for my last rest above 13,000 feet and fall asleep immediately.

Since I prepared everything yesterday, we take advantage of the morning to rest and look at the views from the campsite: the floor of the Barranco valley, the vast plain, and life at the campsite. We watch the porters take down the tents and move off into the distance in single file along the rocky walls, then reappear in mid-morning to quickly erect the tents before the tourists arrive.

After lunch, Simon and I retrace our steps along the path we'd traveled days ago in order to return to the entrance to the national park. Simon sets a slow, steady pace so that we can run down without tiring ourselves. I met him for the first time several months ago, at the Western States 100, where he had greatly impressed me. I was walking in Squaw Valley on the afternoon before the race and encountered him sitting at a table on the terrace. He was clearly very strong, with muscular arms and what I figured to be abdominal muscles made of steel. His hair was jet black and trimmed close to his head. He stood up to say hello, and I had to look up to look him in the eye, not only because I'm quite short, but because the man before me was over six and a half feet tall. Professional habit made me look closely at his legs, and I noticed that every muscle, vein, and sinew stood out under his skin. I felt as if I were in the presence of a 100-meter sprinter, and it amazed me how someone with his physique could run long distances so well and how agile he was on difficult terrain.

His large eyes bulged out of a round, youthful face, and if he hadn't been smiling, he'd have certainly scared me. However, Simon always smiled, always talked about cheerful subjects, and always had a joke or a dance ready to try out on us. It was a piece of good fortune when he agreed to be our guide on my record attempt, because he was able to show me all the paths and surprises, dangers and shortcuts the mountain held in store, as well as how to acclimate. He also let me share in his way of seeing the mountain, of drawing on the energy radiating from the trees and roots, rocks and wind. He knows Kilimanjaro is a very important source of income for his country and his people because it attracts large numbers of tourists who want to climb the African continent's highest peak and provides a lot of work for the region's porters, guides, and traders. However, it is also a source of life, through the water it supplies to its inhabitants to drink and through the trees that oxygenate the air they breathe, and he is aware that they are the most difficult gifts to preserve but the most important to sustain.

As I contemplate the landscape and listen to the stories he tells me about each place we run through, we reach the entrance to the national park and erect our tents for the night. As it is late, we immediately prepare bowls of cream of carrot soup and huge plates of pasta, which I have a hard time finishing. No doubt about it— Simon's six-foot-five frame and my five-foot-six frame need quite different amounts. We slip into our sleeping bags with full stomachs, and I drift off to sleep wondering what tomorrow will bring.

We wake up at dawn and breakfast on pancakes washed down by cups of tea. We have set our camp a few feet from the Umbwe Gate, at an altitude of about 5,000 feet, surrounded by ancient trees that rise like skyscrapers into the clouds. The earth is damp, and the low vegetation, comprising ferns and other kinds of bushes with large leaves, spreads densely over the mud. It is impossible to wander off the path.

At around 7 a.m. we go over to the Umbwe Gate, where part of the team and some park guards are waiting to film and time the run and be present as I attempt to break the record.

The sky looks clear behind a thin layer of clouds, and from Barranco the team confirms that there is a great sea of clouds beneath their feet but that the temperature is good, that it's not very cold at the higher levels. This is great news, since aiming for a record in excellent conditions and dry terrain is easier than if it is raining and the surface is slippery; it's dangerous to run at an altitude of 16,000 feet when you are sopping wet. My legs feel fresh and ready to start uphill.

Lotta begins the countdown, and after she says, "1," I launch off at top speed with Simon, who will accompany me for the part of the course that will take me through the jungle and up to the ceiling of Africa. I feel good and take long, efficient strides, making sure I don't slip on the mud and pushing hard so that I hardly need to lift up my legs. I feel my breathing, strides, and heartbeats synchronizing, and I run through the trees with ease. Simon begins to drop behind. I feel really good and decide I should make the most of every moment to reach 13,000 feet, since later on, even though I am well acclimated, I cannot be sure how my body will respond.

The trail narrows into a path that gradually climbs up through ancient trees, between roots and rocky boulders. The humidity is very high in this stretch. It reminds me of the Mount Kinabalu race in Malaysia, where the humidity is also heavy. Sweat streams down my face, but I feel too good to reduce my pace. I speed on, and in a little over an hour I'm at the first camp on the ascent, at Umbwe

Cave, at nearly 10,000 feet. From here on, there is a spectacular change in vegetation; we leave behind tall, leafy woods and start out on a ridge surrounded by 7-foot-high branches from which hang long yellow beards. It feels like running through a landscape from *The Lord of the Rings*, and I wouldn't be completely surprised to see an elf jump out of these bushes.

When a gap opens up between two of the long beards, we glimpse the magnificent ravines under the ridge that go down to a plain full of healthy vegetation and lofty trees. I imagine that no one has ever set foot in these places that seem inaccessible to humans. And for one or two moments, on the occasional bend in the path, you can see the peak of Kilimanjaro very far off and very high up. When I look at it for the first time, it seems scary. I look at my watch and realize it will be impossible to climb that far in four hours. It's too far and too high. But I am making good—very good—time, am well under the record, and my legs let me drive easily on up the steep slopes.

I return my focus to the miles just ahead of me and accelerate to Barranco. The bearded bushes start to give way to a more barren landscape that's rocky and full of thick volcanic sand, where only a few lobelias and large ragwort manage to live. I've got my music on loud so as not to be too distracted by the landscape or the sounds of nature. It's so fantastic all around me that it would be very easy to be bewitched by nature. So REM, Manel, Blondie, the Black Eyed Peas, and others help me cut myself off a bit from the attractions of nature and to concentrate only on my body and the trail unfolding immediately in front of me. That is why I turn past a tower of lava and don't hear the shouts from Greg, who is waiting with a small camera to immortalize these scenes. He starts to accompany me, running behind me, but I keep accelerating, absorbed in concentration, and I am soon alone again. I have not stopped to think about it, but I am now near 13,000 feet and have yet to note any shortage of oxygen; in fact, I'm running as if I were at 6,500 feet, which means all the acclimating we did the week before has paid off.

Pleased about this, I run at top speed along the rocky path that will bring me to the Barranco Camp plateau that has been my home for the last week. The imposing wall of the summit of Kilimanjaro looms above: 6,500 feet of vertical rock draped by a few remaining glaciers. I again conclude that it will be impossible to reach the top in just over three hours.

My route leads me off the most direct route, to the left, around those walls that can't be crossed and on toward more gentle, northerly slopes. When I reach the camp, Stephan is waiting for me with a canteen of water that I down in one gulp. I set out 2 hours and 15 minutes ago and have drunk nothing since, although I have taken an energy gel every hour.

Without losing any more time, I start running along a path that heads across masses of scree toward Lava Tower, toward a camp that enjoys spectacular views over Mount Meru and where we spent one night while acclimatizing. I keep passing porters coming down from the camp, all of whom cheer and clap as I go by. Although there's no telephone coverage here, it seems that word of mouth is still a very efficient tool of communication: They all know who I am and what I am attempting to do today.

I follow this path for a couple of miles, then take a right turn under a precipitous crest of black rock to reach Glacier Camp, at around 16,000 feet, avoiding Lava Tower and thus saving some 10 minutes. The landscape has now given up on vegetation. Here the path has been carved out among blocks of broken black rock and brown stone that range from the size of dining room tables down to the finest dust. The dirt track slopes down, and my feet slide a few inches with each step I take, sinking between the rocks.

It becomes difficult to make headway, and I realize I am no longer running. My feet feel leaden. *It can't be a shortage of oxygen,* I think. *A couple of days ago, I easily ran up this same slope. Why am I finding it so hard now?* However, I think little of it; I was thousands of feet lower only three hours ago, in the middle of a jungle where my muscles were able to take in all the oxygen they needed. I quickly down a couple of gels but find that I can't accelerate. It can't be a sudden attack of fatigue; I can't have used up all my reserves of strength. I feel sure that my muscles can pump at top speed and are just waiting to thrust me forward. But I feel empty, void of energy. When I manage two or three minutes at a good rate, I have to stop and breathe deeply. My head, too, is navigating in unknown waters. It can't concentrate on my body, on my pace, or on the surrounding landscape. It simply wants this feeling of emptiness to end. It wants to stop, stretch out, and rest.

But no, I can't stop; time keeps moving on. I lift my head and run confidently, strongly, and with determination until I am forced to stop a few minutes later. I can't fathom this situation. I have the strength yet can't draw on it. It is trapped and waiting for an energy tap to be turned on that seems to have jammed.

Time goes by faster than ever, unlike the miles, which are going by more slowly than ever. However, I gradually climb up between two sloping walls of rock and come out onto the enormous crater of the volcano. Here I contemplate one of the most surreal landscapes I have ever seen. There is a great area of black lava sand that, after being exposed to the sun's heat all day with nothing to provide shadow, is so hot that if you sink your hands into it, it is like putting them into boiling water. Huge blocks of ice hang above this beachy landscape, like icebergs that have lost their way and are marooned on a remote island.

The cold wind that blows when I reach the crater rim rouses me, enabling me to break into a run across this desert before I reach the last wall on the climb. My legs feel light once again, and apparently oxygen is back, circulating around me. I make the most of it and stride across the long plateau, smiling, telling myself, *I've done it. I've gotten there.*

However, when I reach the 650-foot wall between myself and Uhuru Peak, my legs immediately feel as though they weigh 200 pounds apiece. The energy tap is switched off again.

I search my iPod for a song to motivate me for this final stretch. I find one and start to feel its electrifying rhythm; the voice and lyrics raise my spirits, releasing me from the weight I'm carrying, and off I run.

I run up over fine sand, sinking down with every step. I still feel energetic, but as the melody moves on, my head wanders and my legs start to feel heavy once again. I try to keep on and not stop until the song ends, but fatigue triumphs over my will and I sit on a rock to rest and take a few deep breaths.

I wait for the song to end and then begin running again, though this time I adopt a long, slow pace until I reach the crest of the summit, where Olivier is waiting. I stretch out on the ground, put my head in my hands, and find myself dozing for a few moments. I wake up almost immediately. *What do you think you are doing?* I demand of myself. *Come on, get up! You've made it. You'll be at the top in a minute, and the suffering stops there.*

I rise and look at my watch: 5 hours and 20 minutes. *Very good!* I think. I break into a gentle canter. The terrain isn't very steep and allows me to recover my strength with each step, to get rid of the heaviness in my legs so that soon I can accelerate, take big strides, and quickly reach the top.

"I've done it! I've done it! Finally!" I say, thinking aloud. I know I will soon be able to execute my usual form on the descent and therefore should beat the record unless there is some unforeseen mishap. I have done the hardest part and now can simply enjoy the descent.

I stop at the top for a few seconds to recoup my strength, drinking from my water canteen and eating cookies. Sònia checks my pulse and the oxygen levels in my blood. Everything is in order. I gaze at the splendid views yet again, and when I feel I have recovered and my head is clear and alert, I get up and start on my long, nonstop descent. I bid farewell to the wind with a loud "Jambo!" and start running over the mass of fine earth that falls from the mountain peak. My legs feel light, my reflexes quick, and my feet go exactly where I want. *Today will be a great day*, I think. *Today will be a wonderful descent.* There's no time to suffer now; there's not even time to run. The time I have left is for flying.

And so I fly, leaping between great blocks of stone and dodging the zigzagging path. I'm going fast, very fast, and the barometer drops quickly. I've run down 3,200 feet in under 15 minutes, and as I leap between the rocks at Barafu Camp, some porters and guides shout out to me, scared that I am falling down the ravines. But I'm not falling; my feet and my body are dancing with the terrain, adapting to its many contours and moving on as quickly as possible, like a rock falling from a mountaintop and ricocheting down, seeking the most direct route. I feel completely in control of my movements and enjoy myself as I have not done for some time. It is as if I could float over this terrain, as if I were skiing over snow. As if I were cycling over a track through the forest. No, I'm even more in control than that. I play with the terrain, tricking it into thinking that I'm going to fall, but then a thousandth of a second before I do, I raise my center of gravity and jump in another direction. Everything goes by at top speed around me: The stones my feet disturb fly past my ear; the stones, walls, sand, and plants rush by under my feet. But it's like being able to bring time to a halt and place myself in a dimension where everything happens slowly. I have plenty of time to dodge each stone that wants to trip me, to steady for a jump, or to swerve before a branch scrapes my body. I'm dancing with the terrain and taking each stride as if it were my last.

The landscape changes again, in the opposite order of my ascent, but now I don't have time to appreciate every new kind of vegetation. In less than an hour I'm at Millennium Camp, where porters who have come to see how my record attempt ends are waiting. I hear them cheering in the distance; they are pleased it's turning out well, and I am pleased for their sake.

I run into the camp in a cloud of dust and stop for a moment to shake out the sand that has gotten into my shoes. The porters have prepared a magnificent jam pancake for me to give me energy for the final part of the descent, and I eat a big chunk. However, I have no time to waste, and a few seconds later I'm back dancing with the rocks and lobelias that litter my path. I am enjoying this descent so much that I don't want it to end.

I leave behind a terrain of big slopes of broken rock and move on to fast paths of huge stone boulders, to esplanades between ragwort and towers of lava and stairways of rock and mud through the wood. After the last encampment, the path becomes a continuous zigzag of muddy stairways of different shapes and sizes. My feet jump two or three steps at a time, always with enough spring to be able to swerve quickly at each turn or to overtake a group of climbers or porters who are making their exhausted way back to civilization. As I pass a group on the right between some enormous trees, I turn around to say hello and wish them a good descent when suddenly I feel my right foot strike a root hard; it doesn't even shift in the ground. My body hurtles forward, and my hands and knees hit the ground several feet farther on. I get up quickly, as if nothing had happened, and look to see if anybody saw me fall. Evidently they did, because the group I was overtaking has stopped a few feet behind me, and they ask me if I am all right.

"I'm fine, everything's okay," I reply as I run off again. My right leg and foot feel numb, and I find it difficult to regain my confident stride. I am intact, apart from some scratches on my hand and a deep cut on my left knee, and I consider myself lucky given the speed I was going. I quickly reestablish a decent rhythm, and my legs start to accelerate when I leave the trail through the woods and come out onto a broader forest track. It's 15 minutes from here to the park's Mweka Gate, and I speed up using as much strength as I can muster, taking increasingly longer and swifter strides. My feet barely touch the ground. My toes only act to power my body forward. I begin to hear noise. Cars that come and go, people shouting and talking, footsteps this way and that. I look at my watch. *Seven hours and 14 minutes. I'm there; one last effort*, I tell myself as I push my legs harder. When I round the next bend, the stone gate that indicates I'm about to leave the park appears a hundred feet in front of me. The rest of my team who didn't climb the mountain are waiting for me behind that gate, along with a number of tourists, guides, and porters who have stayed on to see me come in.

As I run through the gate, I feel a huge surge of emotion, as if it were one of the biggest races I have ever run. But on this occasion, emotion doesn't lead me to replay the moments I experienced on my ascent and descent of Mount Kilimanjaro, nor do I feel the adrenaline and excitement of having beaten the record. Instead, the images rushing into my head are from the whole of our stay on the mountain. The warm conversations with porters, the dances every evening, the first time we climbed to the top, the ginger and hot tea. And looking around, I can see that each member of the team is reliving the same experiences. One individual beats a record, yes, but many help to make it happen.

After this adventure and so many others on various trips around the world—to Japan, Malaysia, Reunion, Argentina, Canada—it's not the results or the records that stay with me. It's the people I have met on the way who, as I was dripping in sweat at the end of a race, waiting for a drug test, sitting with a headlamp on in a tent at 16,000 feet, standing in a Japanese sanctuary surrounded by bonsai, or warming myself by a fireside in a stone refuge, have passed on their knowledge and experience. Together we have seen the same wondrous landscapes and shared the same emotions. Doctors, teachers, guides, fishermen, hunters, nomadic travelers, executives . . . all whose experiences could fill 10 books or more. The words they spoke to me and the emotions we lived together are forever etched in my memory, far more deeply than any victory or record time.

what i think
about when
i think about
running

9

The landscape passes by in a blur on the other side of the window, ensuring my eyes can't focus on any one image and thus freeing my mind to explore my thoughts. I'm sitting on a yellow-and-brown-striped plush seat at the end of an almost empty compartment in a train headed east.

When thoughts sail through my head and can find no way out, I always go for a run to free up my mind. I find that then I can see everything more clearly, and that my problems are put into perspective. Running is the best way for me to disconnect from routine and to find the solutions to my problems, which I struggle to see even though they are often staring me right in the face. I was once told that if I wanted to survey a mountain and find the best path across it, it is better not to be halfway up or at its foot, because the rocks, buttresses, and valleys will hide the other paths from sight. You must distance yourself from the mountain to be able to see it whole. That's why now, when I'm thinking about what I think about when I think about running, I must distance myself from activity, sweat, and effort, and from the emotions that drive me.

I spend my whole life thinking about running: before I start out, I think about how I will run; when I run, I think about how it's going; and afterward I think about how I ran. I try to control it all: my training, whether it has been too much or too little and how much I need in order to be in the best shape; the weather, if it is too cold and if it will affect my next race. I try to control my personal life: whether I will be able to see my friends that weekend or not, because I do or don't have a race; whether my family will be able to come to a race; if dinner with the family will allow the right number of calories I'll need the next day. I try to control my body, listen to my pulse and heartbeats and control them with my thoughts, control whether my breathing is from my chest or my diaphragm. I try to adapt my sleep to whether I need more or less rest.

Nothing is outside my control during a race; I have the route etched on my mind, I know my rivals as if they were brothers, and my body reacts as though it were driven by remote control.

Nevertheless, I often think that however much I have everything under control, however much I might think nothing can escape my micromanagement, there will always be surprises, hurdles to cross. It is at such moments when all my organization is worthless.

But I rarely look back to the past. I've always thought that from the moment something happens, whether it's a problem we'd rather not have experienced or a piece of good news we'd like to enjoy forever, it already belongs to our past. I can't harp on it or regret what I didn't do well or what might have been, because however much I might like to have done it differently, it will never happen, and you pay dearly in competitions for seconds, minutes, or hours you spend lamenting. Competitions have taught me to find the quickest solution to an obstacle, to confront my goals afresh, and to leave the past behind me.

The most difficult thing to control is, of course, what we can't touch, all the ephemeral things our hands can't manipulate. We will never really quite know how our brain works, why we are excited by some things and stressed by others. But mental control is essential in sport if you're going to achieve top results.

How many people say they can't sleep the night before a race because they feel stressed out? How many people in the course of a race lose heart at a mishap, however insignificant it might seem from the outside? How many people feel their world has collapsed because they got a bad result in a race for which they had high hopes?

An ability to keep things in their relative context is what has helped me avoid these kinds of late-night stresses and race catastrophes. If our preparation and training have been good, we should not worry whether we will finish well; if they have not been good, we shouldn't worry either, because we know we *won't* finish well. When we get nervous, when our world starts to collapse, all we can really do is try to do the best we can and hope that intuition will guide us along the right path. And a race is only a race. When we feel stressed, we should ask whether this problem that feels as if it will last forever will seem as huge in 10 years' time or whether we will look back on it as an amusing anecdote.

It is possible to achieve a relaxed state through the body, via meditation, yoga, or breathing, or by going out for a run to let off steam, or with a night out on the town to distance ourselves from our problems for a moment and see them from another perspective. But how long will this state of calm last? How long will it take us to return to our previous state? We can achieve a state of lasting calm only through awareness, by becoming aware of our condition and seeing it from a distance. It isn't about getting one problem off our backs; we must change our way of seeing life.

But this isn't the central question we runners ask ourselves nor the one people who don't run ask us. This is only what I think about in order to be able to run faster, farther, and longer. But *why* do I run? *Why* am I so hooked on competing? I don't know why, and I don't know if there is one reason. I could say that I want to feel my endorphins activating when I get tired, that I long to reexperience the excitement of winning a race or seeing magnificent landscapes. I could say I run because of the feeling of well-being it gives me, because of my health, or in order to disconnect from problems. Perhaps I want to deal with longings I repressed as a child or try to belong to a group, to feel valued in something. Perhaps I do it to pursue my fate or escape my fears. Perhaps it is to rediscover that romantic glow that is lost in life today or to create a dramatic, heroic narrative for myself in the image of legends from wars or the Middle Ages, where I can be the protagonist and hero in a world where it is increasingly difficult to experience the epic.

However, I think I run simply because I like doing it; I enjoy every minute and don't wonder why. I know that when I am running and skiing, my body and mind are in harmony and allow me to feel that I am free, can fly, and can express myself through all my talents. The mountain is a blank canvas, and I'm the paintbrush that refuses to obey a paint-by-number pattern. Running provides my imagination with the means to express itself and delve into my inner self.

I've always been a creative person. I tried my luck with music—playing the cello—but my technique was poor and I never succeeded in overcoming the stiffness I felt with rhythm that was controlled by established codes. Writing gave me greater freedom, since here I had fewer technical handicaps; however, it wouldn't let me disrupt the letters and explore other parts of my imagination. I managed to make more headway with drawing but could seldom finish anything. I always lacked the ability to reach closure, was limited by the techniques and concepts I so wanted to grasp. In the end, I chose sport because I knew the canvas perfectly and was in control of the techniques necessary to explore every goal I set for myself.

A great athlete is one who takes advantage of the ability that genetics have brought him in order to secure great achievements, but an *exceptional* athlete is one who can swim in the waters of complexity and chaos, making what seems difficult easy, creating order from chaos. Creative individuals search for chaos in order to explore all the places they can imagine beyond the frontiers of consciousness, following the irrational forces that come from within themselves and from their environment.

Perhaps I run because I need to feel creative. I need to know what is inside me and then see it realized somewhere outside me. We can explore our inner selves and know what we are capable of, but perhaps we also need to externalize that and separate it out from our bodies in order to view it as spectators, in order to evaluate it and see the defects so that we can do it again, better. It is a pleasure intrinsic to the creation of beauty.

A race is like a work of art; it is a creation that requires not only technique and work but also inspiration to reach a satisfactory outcome. But, also, it is ephemeral, because like a Buddhist mandala, the enjoyment comes in the creating of it; at the moment of climax, at the point when it has reached its perfection, it disappears and will be impossible to create exactly ever again. There can be

no repeats; we can relive similar emotions and experience familiar sensations, but they will never take the same shape, because
inspiration leads us to explore different forms.

From the moment a race no longer exists and we can no longer feel it, it belongs to the past. In order to feel again what we
have experienced, the best we can do is relive those moments.
And reliving an experience, whether it is a race or anything else,
assumes a change of code, a new translation or interpretation, the
elimination of what we don't want to relive and the enhancing of
what we want to cling to, the editing within our memory of the
story we will tell later. This doesn't simply mean getting rid of bad
times and expanding moments of glory; it is about distorting reality. What *is* real and what is imaginary? What proportion of what
we remember or feel is but a part of our dreams? Did these races
and journeys really exist, or are they only the fruits of my whimsical imagination? Photos enable me to confirm that I was there,
and the records mean that in a hundred years it will still be possible to remember how long I took, but I will never know for certain what I was feeling, what excited me, since my eyes aren't a
camera that simply soaks paper with colors; my eyes see what my
brain lets them see, and they distort reality according to my state
of mind. Did Alba really exist? Or was she an oasis in my mind dis-
tracting me from the monotony of running on long cross-country
or mountain hikes? She can't only be the fruit of my imagination.
I fell in love; I suffered in love. It must have been real. However,
I was also able to cry and feel excited when there were only two
hours to go to La Redoute stadium on the Diagonale des Fous,
when I was imagining what I would feel when I crossed the finish
line. The emotion was real enough. I could see and hear the people
around me, could see the grass in the stadium, got goose bumps

and cried because I was so excited, but that vision was displaced in time; it would be what I relived a few hours later when my feet crossed the finish line.

Am I form or content? Are we flesh and blood or feelings and emotions? What is more authentic: a mountain we remember because of its size and height or the distorted image we carry in our feelings when we remember it? Which life is more authentic: our body's or our mind's? I sometimes imagine that we lead two parallel lives that feed on each other, but no, I am sure we can live only one, the one that oscillates between the two. In essence, what sticks in life is what we have lived, what we remember in order to feel the excitement again by reliving it. So what if it becomes distorted at some point? Happiness is a goal of every human being, and it comes to us through small pleasures, big victories, strong emotions, love, and even surviving love, whether experienced by our body, by our imagination, or reformulated by our memory.

I get off the train without any baggage. A curtain of drizzle starts to fall, but the sun is shining just behind the clouds. I cross the tracks as the train moves into the distance, and I head up a trail, zigzagging between the trees that shelter me from the rain. The sun begins to light up the grass and the stones beneath my feet. Scattered drops of rain softly strike my legs and face, and my T-shirt and pants grow heavier. With each step I feel the water slopping up and down in my shoes, but that doesn't hold me back; in fact, it drives me on, makes me run quicker, jump higher. I abandon the track, leaping over small bushes and dancing to the rhythm of the rain. I sing, shouting as loudly as I can into the sky. I am happy, and no one can stop me from smiling.

I run up and down nonstop until I emerge on a treeless plateau. I open my arms, shut my eyes, and tilt my face to the sky, letting the rain wet my face as the wind tries to blow away the drops streaming down my cheeks. I take deep breaths and launch back into a run, jumping and climbing farther up, running faster and faster. There is no boundary, no threshold, nothing that can stop me. I smell the trees, the wet grass, spring, the rich earth, all of which carry the unmistakable aroma of life. I am happy. I stop and rest for a moment, breathing hard, my hands on my knees. I am chasing no one, and no one is chasing me. I think how happiness isn't a destination but rather a path to follow, spending time along that way and postponing its inevitable end.

My skin is cold but my body is warm, and I find that the panting revives me. As I begin to accelerate, my breaths slice out through the bitter cold, and my footprints head off into distant valleys.

ACKNOWLEDGMENTS

To Jordi Canals, Joan Solà, and my family and friends for believing in me from day one and helping me to realize my dreams.

To my Catalan publishing house, Ara Llibres, for giving me this unique opportunity and helping me whenever I needed help.

CREDITS

Color Section Photographs
Page 2: Courtesy of Mónica Dalmasso
Page 3: Courtesy of Stephan Repke
Page 4, top: Courtesy of Mónica Dalmasso
Page 4, bottom: Courtesy of J. P. Clatot
Page 5, top right: Courtesy of Stephan Repke
Page 5, bottom: Courtesy of Miquel Marín
Pages 6–7: Courtesy of Pascal Tournaire
Page 8, top left: Courtesy of Mónica Dalmasso
Page 8, top right: Courtesy of *TrailRunner* magazine
Page 8, bottom: Courtesy of Gustav Arvidsson

Translation
Translated from Catalan by Peter Bush
The translation of this work was supported by a grant from
the Institut Ramon Llull.

LLLL institut
ramon llull
Catalan Language and Culture